Reading
for the
Main Idea

McGraw-Hill Basic Skills
Tools for Learning Success

Dr. Alton L. Raygor, Consulting Editor

STUDY SKILLS	READING	VOCABULARY	SPELLING	WRITING	MATHEMATICS
Yates: LISTENING AND NOTE-TAKING	Fisher: READING TO DISCOVER ORGANIZATION	Davis: BASIC VOCABULARY SKILLS	LTI: BASIC SPELLING SKILLS	LTI: WRITING SKILLS I	Eraut: FUNDAMENTALS OF ARITHMETIC
LTI: LIBRARY SKILLS	Fisher: READING TO UNDERSTAND SCIENCE			LTI: WRITING SKILLS II	Eraut: FUNDAMENTALS OF ELEMENTARY ALGEBRA
Raygor and Wark: SYSTEMS FOR STUDY	Harnadak: CRITICAL READING IMPROVEMENT			LTI: PARAGRAPH PATTERNS	Eraut: FUNDAMENTALS OF INTERMEDIATE ALGEBRA
Samson: PROBLEM SOLVING IMPROVEMENT	Maxwell: SKIMMING AND SCANNING SKILLS				
Wark and Mogen: READ, UNDERLINE, REVIEW	Raygor and Schick: READING AT EFFICIENT RATES				
	Raygor: READING FOR THE MAIN IDEA				
	Raygor: READING FOR SIGNIFICANT FACTS				

Pretests and Posttests are available to measure progress.

Editor's Introduction

This book is one of seven parts in a series devoted to instruction in reading skills. This reading series, in turn, is part of a larger system of instructional materials—McGraw-Hill Basic Skills: Tools for Learning Success. Designed at the University of Minnesota Reading and Study Skills Center, Basic Skills is aimed at college-bound high school students, and junior college and college students who need to improve those skills necessary for academic success. The system consists of *tests* to determine instructional needs and *materials* designed to meet those needs, plus instructor's manuals to explain the tests and materials and the relationship between them. The purpose of the *tests* is to find out what instruction students need in basic skills, and the purpose of the *materials* is to give them that instruction. Each student gets what he or she needs without wasting time on unnecessary tasks.

Six basic skill topics—study, reading, vocabulary, spelling, writing, and mathematics—are covered, and two tests (A and B forms) are provided for each topic. Subscales on the tests are matched to accompanying instructional materials: thus a student with a low score on one or more subscales gets instruction in the corresponding skill. The second form of the test may be used to evaluate progress after instruction.

The materials in Basic Skills have been field-tested and revised to provide the best possible results. While most of the materials are self-instructional programs, the tests, of course, are designed for supervised administration. These testing instruments have been carefully developed and standardized by California Test Bureau. The latest research techniques and procedures have been utilized to ensure the highest possible validity and reliability.

The instructional materials are designed to be used separately, if desired, and can be purchased as single units. Most of the materials are suitable for adoption as textbooks in such basic skill courses as Freshman English, Communications, How to Study, Vocabulary Development, and Remedial or Developmental Mathematics. Individualized diagnosis and instruction are optional in such settings.

This second edition of *Reading for the Main Idea* is designed to retain the best features of the original version, while introducing some new features that will make it more current, easier to use, more interesting and varied, and generally more effective.

The primary goal of the material is to assist students in reading comprehension. While it tends to focus on the main idea or central thought expressed by the author, it provides instruction and practice that will assist in other comprehension subskills.

This second edition is different from the first in several ways. Some of the content material has been dropped because it was out of date, too difficult, or dull. Other, newer material has been added. The program is also structured differently, with more parts and frequent progress checks.

Alton L. Raygor
Consulting Editor
University of Minnesota

Reading for the Main Idea

A Program for
Self-Instruction

Second Edition

ALTON L. RAYGOR
Professor of Educational Psychology
University of Minnesota

McGRAW-HILL BOOK COMPANY
New York   St. Louis   San Francisco
Auckland   Bogotá   Düsseldorf   Johannesburg
London   Madrid   Mexico   Montreal   New Delhi
Panama   Paris   São Paulo   Singapore
Sydney   Tokyo   Toronto

READING FOR THE MAIN IDEA

1234567890   DODO   7832109

Library of Congress Cataloging in Publication Data

Raygor, Alton Lamon, date
   Reading for the main idea.
   "McGraw-Hill basic skills."
   1. Reading comprehension. I. Title.
LB1050.45.R39 1979   428'.4'3   78-10737
ISBN 0-07-044417-X

This book was set in Palatino by A Graphic Method Inc.
The editors were William A. Talkington and Phyllis T. Dulan;
the production supervisor was Joe Campanella.
R. R. Donnelley & Sons Company was printer and binder.

Acknowledgments

Allen, Clark K., James M. Buchanan, and Marshall R. Colberg: *Prices, Income, and Public Policy*, 2d ed., McGraw-Hill Book Company, New York, 1959, pp. 108, 52.

Allendoerfer, Carl B., and Cletus O. Oakley: *Principles of Mathematics*, 2d ed., McGraw-Hill Book Company, New York, 1963, p. 1.

Archer, Jerome W., and Joseph Schwartz: *A Reader for Writers: A Critical Anthology of Prose Readings*, 1st ed., McGraw-Hill Book Company, New York, 1962, pp. 36–37, 187.

Davidoff, Linda L.: *Introduction to Psychology*, McGraw-Hill Book Company, New York, 1976, pp. 4, 12–13.

Freeman, Otis W., and John W. Morris: *World Geography*, 2d ed., McGraw-Hill Book Company, New York, 1964, p. 547.

Gewehr, Wesley M., Donald C. Gordon, David S. Sparks, and Roland N. Stromberg: *The United States: A History of Democracy*, 2d ed., McGraw-Hill Book Company, New York, 1960, pp. 50, 84, 145, 6, 19, 520.

Green, Arnold W.: *Sociology: An Analysis of Life in Modern Society*, 4th ed., McGraw-Hill Book Company, New York, 1964, pp. 48, 41.

Hackett, Herbert, and William Baker: *Of Studies: Reading and Writing*, 1st ed., McGraw-Hill Book Company, New York, 1960, p. 64.

Hackett, Laura, and Richard Williamson: *Anatomy of Reading*, 1st ed., McGraw-Hill Book Company, New York, 1965, p. 144.

Hill, J. Ben, Lee O. Overholts, Henry W. Popp, and Alvin R. Grove, Jr.: *Botany: A Textbook for Colleges*, 3d ed., McGraw-Hill Book Company, New York, 1960, pp. 34, 117.

Hoebel, E. Adamson, Jesse D. Jennings, and Elmer R. Smith: *Readings in Anthropology*, 1st ed., McGraw-Hill Book Company, New York, 1955, p. 47.

Hurlock, Elizabeth B.: *Child Growth and Development*, 2d ed., McGraw-Hill Book Company, New York, 1956, pp. 123, 119.

Hussey, Russell C.: *Historical Geology: The Geologic History of North America*, 2d ed., McGraw-Hill Book Company, New York, 1949, pp. 5, 10.

Johns, Edward B., Wilfred C. Sutton, and Lloyd E. Webster: *Health for Effective Living*, 3d ed., McGraw-Hill Book Company, New York, 1962, pp. 46, 483, 15, 37.

Kamien, Roger: *Music: An Appreciation*, McGraw-Hill Book Company, New York, 1976, pp. 3, 72, 507, 513.

Koeppe, Clarence E., and George C. De Long: *Weather and Climate*, McGraw-Hill Book Company, New York, 1958, pp. 263, 89.

Lazarus, Richard S.: *Adjustment and Personality*, 1st ed., McGraw-Hill Book Company, New York, 1961, p. 4.

Morgan, Clifford T., and Richard A. King: *Introduction to Psychology*, 5th ed., McGraw-Hill Book Company, 1975, pp. 216, 231.

Morgan, Clifford T.: *Introduction to Psychology*, 2d ed., McGraw-Hill Book Company, New York, 1961, pp. 301, 605.

Myers, Bernard S.: *Art and Civilization*, 1st ed., McGraw-Hill Book Company, New York, 1957, p. 2.

Ratner, Leonard G.: *Music: The Listener's Art*, 1st ed., McGraw-Hill Book Company, New York, 1957, pp. 130, 287.

Reid, Loren: *Speaking Well*, 3d ed., McGraw-Hill Book Company, New York, 1977, pp. 124, 93.

Richardson, Robert S.: *The Fascinating World of Astronomy*, McGraw-Hill Book Company, New York, 1960, pp. 36, 200, 35.

Robinson, Halbert B., and Nancy M. Robinson: *The Mentally Retarded Child: A Psychological Approach*, 1st ed., McGraw-Hill Book Company, New York, 1965, p. 241.

Rodee, Carlton C., Totton J. Anderson, and Carl Q. Christol: *Introduction to Political Science*, 1st ed., McGraw-Hill Book Company, New York, 1957, pp. 20, 10, 118, 79, 60, 147, 57.

Samuelson, Paul A.: *Economics: An Introductory Analysis*, 6th ed., McGraw-Hill Book Company, New York, 1964, pp. 21, 37.

Sanders, Donald H.: *Computers in Society*, 2d ed., McGraw-Hill Book Company, New York, 1977, pp. 70, 79, 41–42.

Smith, Alpheus W., and John N. Cooper: *Elements of Physics*, 7th ed., McGraw-Hill Book Company, New York, 1964, p. 29.

Sorenson, Herbert: *Psychology in Education*, 2d ed., McGraw-Hill Book Company, New York, 1948, pp. 80–81, 131, 357, 54, 77, 38, 254, 46, 442.

Stagner, Ross: *Psychology of Personality*, 2d ed., McGraw-Hill Book Company, New York, 1948, pp. 85, 11.

Storer, Tracy I., Robert L. Usinger, James W. Nybakken, and Robert C. Stebbins: *Elements of Zoology*, 4th ed., McGraw-Hill Book Company, New York, 1977, p. 93.

Storer, Tracy I., and Robert L. Usinger: *General Zoology*, 4th ed., McGraw-Hill Book Company, New York, 1965, pp. 56, 208, 209.

Weisz, Paul B.: *Elements of Biology*, 1st ed., McGraw-Hill Book Company, New York, 1961, p. 5, 49, 116, 2, 164, 50.

Contents

EDITOR'S INTRODUCTION   iii

NOTE TO THE STUDENT   xi

PART 1: INTRODUCTION TO THE MAIN IDEA   1

PART 2: RECOGNIZING THE MAIN IDEA   11

PROGRESS CHECK NUMBER ONE   53

PART 3: MORE PRACTICE RECOGNIZING THE MAIN IDEA   55

PART 4: WORKING WITH THE MAIN IDEA   77

PROGRESS CHECK NUMBER TWO   99

PART 5: MORE PRACTICE WORKING WITH THE MAIN IDEA   101

REVIEW   131

PART 6: STATING THE MAIN IDEA   133

A FINAL NOTE TO THE STUDENT   159

Note to the Student

The primary task in reading is to understand exactly what the author is trying to say. In spite of the importance of this task, many readers, even very good readers, fail to get the main idea of the material they are reading. This is not because getting the main idea is a difficult task, but rather because most people have had little practice or training in understanding the main idea and simply do not bother to do it. This is especially true in study-type reading where students often concentrate on the trees and fail to notice the forest; that is, they are paying such close attention to the details of a passage that they do not see the main point the author is trying to make. Evidence from research studies has shown that knowing the main idea of a passage makes it easier not only to understand the details of the passage but also *to remember them*. The purpose of this book, then, is to give you training and practice in recognizing and understanding the main idea of a written passage so that in the future you will be able to do this on your own, quickly and easily.

What Is the Main Idea?
Probably the easiest way to understand the meaning of "main idea" is to think of this question: If this author had to boil this passage down to a single, brief statement, what would it be? For example, look at the following passage:

It is estimated that in 1850 there were over a million and a half grizzly bears in the United States. By 1950 there were less than 500. The remaining grizzlies are concentrated in a few small areas, mostly in zoos and high in the Rockies. Their number continues to dwindle as the result of hunting, poisoning, destruction of their natural habitat, and competition with human beings for food and living space. It remains to be seen whether the grizzly bear will survive this onslaught or will be added permanently to the list of animals that once lived on the earth.

Although the passage contains a lot of information, the *main idea* is that *grizzly bears are in danger of extinction and there are far fewer of them than there used to be.*

As another example, you might look back to the first paragraph of this section and note that the main idea is that *many people do not understand the main idea of passages they read even though understanding the main idea is very important and not very difficult.*

Very simply stated, then, the main idea is the main point the author is trying to make.

Common Mistakes in Analyzing the Main Idea

Students make three basic mistakes in analyzing the main idea of a reading passage:

1. They get a vague, general notion of what the author is saying without understanding the main point. For example, you might state the main idea of the passage on grizzly bears as *the history and life of the grizzly bear.* Obviously this is *too general* since there are many things about the life and history of the grizzly bear that the author does not discuss in the passage.
2. They mistake a fact, example, or single statement from a passage for the main idea. This is probably the most common mistake made. It happens when a small part of a passage is taken to be the main idea. You might state the main idea of the grizzly bear passage as *in 1850 there were over a million and a half grizzly bears in the United States.* Clearly this is *too specific* and refers only to part of what the author is trying to say.
3. They introduce irrelevant ideas that the author never intended. This error often occurs when the reader is familiar with the topic of a passage and reads into it things which fit with the topic even though the author never mentions them. For example, you might state the main idea of the grizzly bear passage as *grizzly bears often attack human beings.* Obviously this is *irrelevant* since the author never mentions anything about grizzlies attacking human beings, and the idea has nothing to do with the main point of the passage.

Organization of the Book

This book is divided into six parts. The first part shows you how you will be working the exercises in the following parts. Parts 2 and 3 provide you with practice in recognizing the main idea. Parts 4 and 5 involve working with the main ideas of paragraphs which are a little more difficult. Finally, in Part 6, you will be reading passages, stating the main idea in your own words, and then comparing your statement with the one in the book. The passages are all taken from textbooks so that they will be very similar to material you will study on your own in the future. In addition, your working material includes a tally card that will help you keep track of your progress.

Alton L. Raygor

Reading
for the
Main Idea

Part 1:
Introduction to the Main idea

The first sixteen practice exercises explain the notion of the main idea and give further information about the types of errors you should avoid. Before you begin to work the exercises, turn to page 3. Notice that the page is divided into four sections printed like regular paragraphs. You read down the page as you would normally do. Flipping through the pages will show you that all right-hand pages through Part 5 are organized in this way. The exercises themselves are made up of questions similar to those on comprehension tests.

Directions for Working the Exercises
You will need an answer sheet on which to work your answers. On a sheet of paper (preferably lined), number from 1 to 16 vertically, leaving room for your answer after each number:

1.
2.
3.
etc.

Now turn to page 2, and read the paragraph. Answer question 1 on page 3 (keep the other questions covered with the card provided with this book) by selecting the alternative (a, b, c, or d) that you think is correct and marking your choice on the top line of your answer sheet. Check your answer immediately by uncovering the correct answer (printed below the responses to the question) and comparing it with the letter on your answer sheet. If you are correct, go to the next question. If you are not correct, put a large "X" through your letter on the answer sheet and write in the correct letter before answering the next question. Do exercises 2 through 16 now.

One of the many skills a good reader develops is the ability to recognize and understand the main idea or central thought of material he has read. The term "main idea," as it is used in these exercises, refers to a statement which summarizes a paragraph. The topic of a well-organized paragraph is often stated in one sentence. Usually, but not always, the topic sentence is the first one in the paragraph. The main idea is not simply the topic sentence. There are other sentences which qualify, or expand, or in some way develop the topic. These are called "supporting sentences." The main idea is expressed in a single statement which summarizes all the ideas in the paragraph, not just some of them. In these exercises, "main idea" means a statement which includes the ideas in the topic sentence as well as the ideas in the supporting sentences.

1. The topic sentence in a paragraph is most often found
    a. At the end of the paragraph
    b. At the beginning of the paragraph
    c. In the middle of the paragraph
    d. In the following paragraph

Answer: b. At the beginning of the paragraph

2. In a well-organized paragraph there is (are) usually _____ main idea(s) or central thought(s).
    a. Two
    b. One
    c. One in each sentence
    d. None

Answer: b. One

3. The best possible summary statement will cover the supporting sentences in addition to the _____ sentence.
    a. First
    b. Last
    c. Longest
    d. Topic

Answer: d. Topic

4. In these exercises, the statement which best summarizes the topic sentence and the supporting sentences is called the _____.
    a. Summary
    b. Main idea
    c. Statement
    d. Topic

Answer: b. Main idea

Sometimes a summary statement can be too general. In a well-organized paragraph, there should be a topic sentence and some supporting sentences. If a summary of any given paragraph contains the ideas of the topic and supporting sentences, we call it the "main idea." If a statement contains more than it should, we say that it is too general. In these exercises a statement is too general if it goes beyond the information given in the paragraph. A statement can also be so vague that it cannot be determined whether or not the ideas in the paragraph are represented. For example, in a paragraph about the Civil War a summary statement which merely refers to American history would be marked too general. For a paragraph about the mako shark a statement which covered all sharks would be marked too general because it would extend beyond (i.e., to all sharks) the specific topic under discussion (i.e., mako sharks).

5. This paragraph describes a kind of summary statement which is
   a. Too specific
   b. Too general
   c. The topic sentence
   d. Irrelevant

Answer: b. Too general

6. A statement which is "too general" is one which is
   a. Vague or overgeneralized
   b. Too concerned with detail
   c. False
   d. Irrelevant

Answer: a. Vague or overgeneralized

7. A good summary statement covers
   a. The topic sentence and the supporting sentences
   b. Only overall categories
   c. Only specific facts
   d. More ideas than the paragraph contains

Answer: a. The topic sentence and the supporting sentences

8. In these exercises, a statement of the main idea which is too vague
   or overgeneralized is called
   a. The main idea
   b. Too general
   c. Too specific
   d. Irrelevant

Answer: b. Too general

A common error in summarizing a paragraph is to pick out an idea that is too specific. Well-organized paragraphs will have a topic sentence and several sentences containing supporting facts. The best statement of the main idea will contain some mention of both the topic sentence and the supporting sentences. However, a statement sometimes mentions only one of the parts of the paragraph or refers to only one detail. Such statements will often appear in these exercises. For example, you may read a paragraph in which the topic is the characteristics of various breeds of hunting dogs. In the paragraph several breeds are evaluated. In these exercises a statement that mentioned only Irish Setters would be too specific. A statement that is concerned with just one specific part of the paragraph should be marked "too specific."

9. This paragraph discusses a kind of incorrect summary statement
   that is
   a. Too general
   b. Too specific
   c. The main idea
   d. Irrelevant

Answer: *b.* Too specific

10. A statement that is "too specific" is wrong because it
    a. Brings in things not mentioned in the paragraph
    b. Is too general or vague
    c. Summarizes only part of the paragraph
    d. Deals in only overall categories

Answer: *c.* Summarizes only part of the paragraph

11. A statement that represents only a specific example rather than the main
    idea would be
    a. Too specific
    b. Too general
    c. Irrelevant
    d. Correct

Answer: *a.* Too specific

12. In these main idea exercises, a statement which is incomplete or
    which deals with only some of the specific ideas covered in the
    paragraph is called
    a. The main idea
    b. Irrelevant
    c. Too general
    d. Too specific

Answer: *d.* Too specific

A well-organized paragraph will not contain any sentences that do not contribute to the idea the author wants to get across. An adequate statement of the main idea will cover only the ideas presented in the paragraph. If a statement covers any ideas not presented in the paragraph, it is *irrelevant*. The ideas in the statement may be related to the main idea of the paragraph, but unless the idea in the statement were actually discussed in the paragraph, it is irrelevant. For example, a statement describing methods of planting corn which read "Corn has many valuable vitamins" would be irrelevant unless the paragraph also covered nutrition. The statement was about the same broad subject as the paragraph, but the idea discussed in the statement is irrelevant to the main idea of the paragraph. If a statement contains ideas which are not actually part of the paragraph, you should mark it "irrelevant."

13. This paragraph discusses a kind of summary statement which is
    a. The main idea
    b. Too general
    c. Irrelevant
    d. Too specific

Answer: *c.* Irrelevant

14. A statement which is "irrelevant" is incorrect because it
    a. Brings in material not covered in the paragraph
    b. Is too vague
    c. Is too detailed
    d. Does not include the topic sentence

Answer: *a.* Brings in material not covered in the paragraph

15. A well-organized paragraph contains a topic sentence and other relevant sentences. It should not include any sentences which are irrelevant to the
    a. Reader's thought
    b. Central thought or main idea
    c. Previous paragraph
    d. Meanings of key words

Answer: *b.* Central thought or main idea

16. In these exercises, a statement of the main idea which brings in ideas not included in the paragraph should be called
    a. The main idea
    b. Too general
    c. Too specific
    d. Irrelevant

Answer: *d.* Irrelevant

Part 2:
Recognizing the Main Idea

When you have finished working exercises 1 to 16, total your errors. If you had trouble working the exercises, reread "Note to the Student" before continuing.

You should answer the following questions in the same way as you answered the practice questions, using answer sheets numbered 17 to 96. In addition, you should keep track of your errors on the tally card you have been using to cover the correct answers. This record will help you evaluate your progress and will be used later either to refer you to specific sections to review if you need additional practice or to allow you to advance if you make only a few or no errors.

Do exercises 17 to 96 now. Every time you make an error, circle the number of the incorrectly answered question on the tally card under the appropriate headings.

If you have any questions, ask your instructor.

You may have noticed that when you see a rainbow you always have your back to the sun. In the morning, when the sun is in the eastern sky, rainbows always appear in the west. In the afternoon they are always in the eastern sky. Rainbows are always in the opposite direction from the sun.

Select the answer which best describes the statement as a summary of the main idea of the paragraph you have just read.

17. Rainbows are always pretty.
    a. Too general
    b. Too specific
    c. Main idea
    d. Irrelevant

Answer: d. Irrelevant. There is no mention in the paragraph of the beauty of a rainbow.

18. Rainbows always appear in the sky in the opposite direction from the sun.
    a. Too general
    b. Too specific
    c. Main idea
    d. Irrelevant

Answer: c. Main idea

19. In the morning rainbows always appear in the western sky.
    a. Too general
    b. Too specific
    c. Main idea
    d. Irrelevant

Answer: b. Too specific. The paragraph explains more than this particular position of a rainbow.

20. Rainbows always appear in a particular relationship to the sun.
    a. Too general
    b. Too specific
    c. Main idea
    d. Irrelevant

Answer: a. Too general. The paragraph tells exactly what pattern rainbows follow.

Wind is simply moving air. Of course, at some times the air moves much faster than at other times. The wind may be only a gentle breeze; it may be a very strong breeze; it may be a gale.

21. High winds cause damage.
    a. Too general
    b. Too specific
    c. Main idea
    d. Irrelevant

Answer: d. Irrelevant. There is no mention in the paragraph of land damage.

22. Wind is simply air moving at various speeds.
    a. Too general
    b. Too specific
    c. Main idea
    d. Irrelevant

Answer: c. Main idea

23. A gentle breeze is very refreshing in hot weather.
    a. Too general
    b. Too specific
    c. Main idea
    d. Irrelevant

Answer: d. Irrelevant. There is no mention in the paragraph of how refreshing summer breezes are.

24. Gales are very fast moving winds.
    a. Too general
    b. Too specific
    c. Main idea
    d. Irrelevant

Answer: b. Too specific. This sentence refers to just a specific type of wind, not to the main idea of wind's being air moving at various speeds.

People used to tell the time of day by shadows. They used sundials to do so. In some sundials it was the length of a shadow which told the time of day. In some sundials it was the position of the shadow. Some sundials are still in use.

25. Sundials look nice in gardens.
    a. Too general
    b. Too specific
    c. Main idea
    d. Irrelevant

Answer: *d.* Irrelevant. There is no mention in the paragraph that sundials look nice.

26. By using sundials, people used to tell the time of day by the length or position of shadows.
    a. Too general
    b. Too specific
    c. Main idea
    d. Irrelevant

Answer: *c.* Main idea. This contains the relevant material from the sentences of the paragraph.

27. In the past sundials were used to tell time.
    a. Too general
    b. Too specific
    c. Main idea
    d. Irrelevant

Answer: *a.* Too general. The paragraph explains *how* a sundial was used to tell time.

28. Sundials, which tell the time of day by the length or position of shadows, were once used to tell time.
    a. Too general
    b. Too specific
    c. Main idea
    d. Irrelevant

Answer: *c.* Main idea. This summarizes the main idea.

Scientists have found out what causes eclipses. The moon travels around the earth. An eclipse of the sun is caused when the moon passes between us and the sun. An eclipse of the moon is caused when the moon travels into the earth's shadow.

29. As the moon travels around the earth, it causes an eclipse of the sun by passing in front of it or an eclipse of the moon by passing into the earth's shadow.
    a. Too general
    b. Too specific
    c. Main idea
    d. Irrelevant

Answer: c. Main idea

30. An eclipse of the sun occurs when the moon passes between the earth and the sun.
    a. Too general
    b. Too specific
    c. Main idea
    d. Irrelevant

Answer: b. Too specific. The paragraph explains the causes of eclipses of both the moon and the sun.

31. Scientists study the movement of the moon and the earth and can predict where each will be at any given time.
    a. Too general
    b. Too specific
    c. Main idea
    d. Irrelevant

Answer: d. Irrelevant. There is no mention in the paragraph of scientists' predicting the positions of the earth and the moon.

32. Scientists have discovered what causes eclipses.
    a. Too general
    b. Too specific
    c. Main idea
    d. Irrelevant

Answer: a. Too general. The paragraph tells exactly what scientists have found the cause of eclipses to be.

Blue dye is only one of the many chemicals that are changed by light. Any chemical which is changed by light is said to be "sensitive to light." If there were no light-sensitive chemicals, we would not be able to take pictures.

33. Without light-sensitive chemicals, we could not take pictures.
    a. Too general
    b. Too specific
    c. Main idea
    d. Irrelevant

Answer: b. Too specific. This statement gives information about the use of light-sensitive chemicals, but does not explain what they are.

34. Dyes are chemicals.
    a. Too general
    b. Too specific
    c. Main idea
    d. Irrelevant

Answer: a. Too general. The paragraph explains that dyes are a certain kind of chemical.

35. Blue dye is a light-sensitive chemical.
    a. Too general
    b. Too specific
    c. Main idea
    d. Irrelevant

Answer: b. Too specific. This statement is concerned with one example, rather than with all light-sensitive chemicals.

36. If a chemical such as blue dye is changed by light, it is said to be "light-sensitive" and may be used in taking pictures.
    a. Too general
    b. Too specific
    c. Main idea
    d. Irrelevant

Answer: c. Main idea

In the early days of our big city post offices, much time was wasted in getting mail from the main station to the substations and from stations to trains. Compressed air then came to be used in many cities to speed up the moving of mail from place to place. Long tubes were built underground. Hollow containers were made to fit into these tubes. Mail was put into the containers, the containers were placed in the tubes, and compressed air was used to shoot the containers through the tubes. Some cities still have many miles of mail tubes. Smaller tubes like the mail tubes are used in many stores, libraries, and factories. They carry money, book slips, orders, and messages from place to place.

37. Some of our cities still have many miles of mail tubes in use every day in post offices.
    a. Too general
    b. Too specific
    c. Main idea
    d. Irrelevant

Answer: b. Too specific. This is a summary of only one part of the paragraph.

38. Compressed air has many valuable commercial uses in addition to being employed in compressed-air tubes.
    a. Too general
    b. Too specific
    c. Main idea
    d. Irrelevant

Answer: d. Irrelevant. There is no mention of other uses of compressed air in the paragraph.

39. Compressed-air tubes are used in stores, libraries, and factories, as well as in post offices.
    a. Too general
    b. Too specific
    c. Main idea
    d. Irrelevant

Answer: b. Too specific. This merely lists some of the places where compressed-air tubes are used, instead of explaining their function and construction.

40. Compressed air is blown through small tubes to move objects to various parts of a building and through larger tubes to move mail containers across a city.
    a. Too general
    b. Too specific
    c. Main idea
    d. Irrelevant

Answer: c. Main idea

Nitrogen is sometimes called a "lazy" gas. There are not any very interesting experiments that can be done with this gas. It is, however, important. We are not built to live in pure oxygen. The nitrogen weakens the oxygen so that the air is right for us. The nitrogen serves the same purpose in the air that water serves in lemonade. Lemonade made of pure lemon juice and sugar would be too strong to be pleasant. To keep the lemonade from being too strong, we add water.

41. All the nitrogen we breathe in we breathe out again.
    a. Too general
    b. Too specific
    c. Main idea
    d. Irrelevant

Answer: d. Irrelevant. There is no direct mention in the paragraph of the breathing of nitrogen.

42. We cannot live in pure oxygen.
    a. Too general
    b. Too specific
    c. Main idea
    d. Irrelevant

Answer: b. Too specific. The paragraph explains how nitrogen weakens the oxygen.

43. Nitrogen is important because it dilutes oxygen so that the air is right for us.
    a. Too general
    b. Too specific
    c. Main idea
    d. Irrelevant

Answer: c. Main idea

44. Besides lemon and sugar, good lemonade needs water.
    a. Too general
    b. Too specific
    c. Main idea
    d. Irrelevant

Answer: b. Too specific. The paragraph mentions lemonade only as an analogy to air.

Motion pictures are simply separate pictures that are shown to you so fast by means of a motion picture machine that you do not see any break between the separate pictures.

45. Motion pictures are a relatively new form of entertainment.
    a. Too general
    b. Too specific
    c. Main idea
    d. Irrelevant

Answer: d. Irrelevant. There is no mention in the paragraph that motion pictures are a new form of entertainment.

46. Motion pictures are separate pictures shown to you so fast that no break occurs between them.
    a. Too general
    b. Too specific
    c. Main idea
    d. Irrelevant

Answer: c. Main idea. This summarizes the paragraph's explanation of a motion picture.

47. Motion pictures are really separate pictures.
    a. Too general
    b. Too specific
    c. Main idea
    d. Irrelevant

Answer: b. Too specific. This statement does not explain how the separate pictures are combined to make a motion picture.

48. A motion picture is a series of separate pictures shown rapidly, with no visible time gaps between them.
    a. Too general
    b. Too specific
    c. Main idea
    d. Irrelevant

Answer: c. Main idea

In school children want the right to do their own thinking and to express themselves freely. They do not like to be governed by rules and regulations whose purpose they do not understand. But fundamentally neither do they like a school where there is so much freedom that there is disorder. They find fault with a teacher in whose room the children are disorderly. They also find fault with teachers who are unimaginative and too rigid and who cannot enjoy a joke. Apparently a schoolroom and a school where behavior is governed largely by understanding and good will afford the freedom that is most satisfying to both pupils and teachers.

49. Children want freedom.
    a. Too general
    b. Too specific
    c. Main idea
    d. Irrelevant

Answer: a. Too general. This statement needs qualification because the use of the word "freedom" is too broad.

50. A firm but understanding teacher can stimulate children to behave properly even in their own homes.
    a. Too general
    b. Too specific
    c. Main idea
    d. Irrelevant

Answer: d. Irrelevant. The paragraph is concerned with the classroom situation only—not the home.

51. Children would appreciate most a classroom in which a firm but liberal atmosphere exists.
    a. Too general
    b. Too specific
    c. Main idea
    d. Irrelevant

Answer: c. Main idea

52. Children do not like a classroom situation in which their teacher is extremely lenient.
    a. Too general
    b. Too specific
    c. Main idea
    d. Irrelevant

Answer: b. Too specific. This statement fails to mention that children do not like an overly strict teacher either.

It is said that teachers should teach children and not subjects. They must do both. Good education is not a matter of the one or the other. A teacher can be so dominated by a desire to teach the subject-matter content that she does not sense what she and her methods are doing to the feelings and attitudes of the children. On the other hand, the teacher should be excellent in the sense that the children not only acquire skills and knowledge but also develop well emotionally. It is possible for her to be skillful not only in developing the children's ability to get along with others, to overcome their fears, and to be happy but also in teaching the subject matter. In practice, subject-matter teaching and child teaching can go hand in hand; and it is more usual for a teacher to be successful in both than in one alone. One can be distrustful of an educational situation in which, figuratively and literally, the pupils are on one side of the desk and the teacher on the other. If the children feel that the school situations are fair and impartial, that working diligently is worthwhile and satisfying, and that the teacher is their friend rather than a taskmaster, one may be reasonably sure that they are in an environment conducive to good mental hygiene and good personal development.

53. In the instruction of youth the ability to teach subject matter and understanding the children in the class are equally important.
    a. Too general
    b. Too specific
    c. Main idea
    d. Irrelevant

Answer: c. Main idea

54. Some teachers concentrate too much on presentation of subject matter in their classes.
    a. Too general
    b. Too specific
    c. Main idea
    d. Irrelevant

Answer: b. Too specific. This statement refers to only one aspect of the paragraph.

55. The education of children includes a variety of teaching skills.
    a. Too general
    b. Too specific
    c. Main idea
    d. Irrelevant

Answer: a. Too general. This statement is not specific enough to the main thought of the paragraph.

56. Teachers should devote more class time to science and mathematics than to literature and social science.
    a. Too general
    b. Too specific
    c. Main idea
    d. Irrelevant

Answer: d. Irrelevant. The paragraph does not discuss which subjects should be taught.

One of the best ways to prevent forgetting is to learn thoroughly. That which is barely learned is rapidly forgotten. [That is,] material on which the hold is weak will be quickly forgotten. The learning should be carried beyond this stage, so that the facts, information, and ideas are thoroughly understood and firmly retained. Just as one drives a stake deep so that it is firm, ties a rope with an extra knot, drives in an extra nail, and, in general, exercises extra care to prevent loosening, so, to prevent forgetting, the learner should study and review the material until it is firmly and thoroughly acquired.

57. Students should study and review material until it is thoroughly learned in order to prevent forgetting.
  a. Too general
  b. Too specific
  c. Main idea
  d. Irrelevant

Answer: c. Main idea

58. A stake must be driven deep so that it will be firm.
  a. Too general
  b. Too specific
  c. Main idea
  d. Irrelevant

Answer: b. Too specific. The paragraph uses the stake as a symbol for all kinds of learning.

59. It helps if students enjoy their work.
  a. Too general
  b. Too specific
  c. Main idea
  d. Irrelevant

Answer: d. Irrelevant. The paragraph makes no mention of enjoyment.

60. Students should study harder.
  a. Too general
  b. Too specific
  c. Main idea
  d. Irrelevant

Answer: a. Too general. This statement does not account for the importance of reviewing in the processes of learning and retention.

The pitch of a sound is decided by the frequency of its vibrations. The faster the vibrations, the higher the pitch; the slower the vibrations, the lower the pitch. Vibration frequency is measured in cycles per second. On a piano the highest frequency tone is 4,186 cycles per second, while the lowest is about 27 cycles per second.

61. High-pitched tones are very difficult to hear.
    a. Too general
    b. Too specific
    c. Main idea
    d. Irrelevant

Answer: d. Irrelevant. The paragraph says nothing about tones that are hard to hear.

62. Lower-pitched sounds often sound louder than higher-pitched sounds.
    a. Too general
    b. Too specific
    c. Main idea
    d. Irrelevant

Answer: d. Irrelevant. The paragraph makes no mention of the loudness of sounds.

63. On a piano the highest frequency tone is 4,186 cycles per second.
    a. Too general
    b. Too specific
    c. Main idea
    d. Irrelevant

Answer: b. Too specific. This is just an example of a high-pitched tone.

64. Which of the following is the main idea?
    a. The piano produces both high- and low-pitched tones.
    b. The pitch of a tone is related to how loud it sounds.
    c. Frequency of vibration is measured in cycles per second; high-pitched tones have greater frequencies than lower-pitched tones.
    d. The pitch of a tone is decided by the frequency of its vibrations.

Answer: c.

Irony is a tone adopted by many writers (and speakers, for that matter) who are critical of what they see. It may take many forms, but when there is a discrepancy between things as they really are and things as they are described, the writing is generally ironic. The boy who sees the pouring rain, the tire of his car flat, and his class already under way when he gets there and who then remarks, "What a wonderful day," has used irony to express his feelings.

65. An example of "irony" would be labeling a cold, rainy day a "beautiful day."
    a. Too general
    b. Too specific
    c. Main idea
    d. Irrelevant

Answer: b. Too specific. This statement is drawn from only one example in the paragraph and ignores other material given.

66. Irony is a way of speaking or writing that conveys a description of things different from what they really are.
    a. Too general
    b. Too specific
    c. Main idea
    d. Irrelevant

Answer: c. Main idea

67. Irony is a tone adopted by certain writers and speakers.
    a. Too general
    b. Too specific
    c. Main idea
    d. Irrelevant

Answer: a. Too general. The paragraph explains exactly what kind of tone irony is.

68. Irony adds enjoyment to literature for a great many people.
    a. Too general
    b. Too specific
    c. Main idea
    d. Irrelevant

Answer: d. Irrelevant. Again, there is no mention in the paragraph about the effect of irony on readers.

Much remains to be learned concerning the inheritance of specific mental traits. Present evidence indicates that the mental potential or native intelligence is hereditarily determined and that the environment determines the extent to which this potential is realized. Studies on identical twins compared with fraternal twins show the importance of heredity. There is evidence that when an individual is well motivated and has ample opportunity, intelligence quotients can be slightly improved. Similarly, an unfavorable and culturally impoverished environment may limit the extent to which mental potential is developed and utilized.

69. Intelligence quotients can be improved by early training and strict discipline.
    a. Too general
    b. Too specific
    c. Main idea
    d. Irrelevant

Answer: d. Irrelevant. There is no mention of either "early training" or "strict discipline" in the paragraph.

70. Present evidence indicates that, although mental potential or intelligence is hereditarily determined, it can be slightly improved or limited by environmental conditions.
    a. Too general
    b. Too specific
    c. Main idea
    d. Irrelevant

Answer: c. Main idea

71. Studies on identical twins compared with fraternal twins show the importance of heredity in determining mental potential.
    a. Too general
    b. Too specific
    c. Main idea
    d. Irrelevant

Answer: b. Too specific. This summary fails to mention the role played by environment.

72. Inherited characteristics can be altered by environmental conditions.
    a. Too general
    b. Too specific
    c. Main idea
    d. Irrelevant

Answer: a. Too general. The paragraph is more specific with regard to the characteristics and factors involved.

To a large extent our course through life is one in which we try to move in the path of pleasure and avoid pain. We seek out people who are pleasant and cordial, and we avoid those who are unpleasant and whom we do not like. Much of the boy-girl, man-woman relationship is determined by pleasure and happiness, and it is unhappiness and pain that spoil the relationship for many. People devote almost unlimited time and money seeking pleasure and happiness, so much so that the entertainment business is one of the biggest in the world. People spend billions for motion pictures, concerts, ball games, horse races, hunting, motoring, and traveling in the pursuit of pleasure. If we add to this the amount spent for medical and dental treatment to eliminate pain, the total becomes almost unbelievably large.

73. An extraordinary amount of money is spent on entertainment.
    a. Too general
    b. Too specific
    c. Main idea
    d. Irrelevant

Answer: b. Too specific. The main concern of the paragraph is the reason for this expenditure, not simply that the money is spent.

74. In almost all facets of life, people strive to achieve pleasure and eliminate pain.
    a. Too general
    b. Too specific
    c. Main idea
    d. Irrelevant

Answer: c. Main idea

75. Reading books is a better leisure-time activity than going to the movies.
    a. Too general
    b. Too specific
    c. Main idea
    d. Irrelevant

Answer: d. Irrelevant. The paragraph is not concerned with the merits of different kinds of entertainment.

76. Much of the success of boy-girl relationships depends on the amount of pleasure derived by the individuals involved.
    a. Too general
    b. Too specific
    c. Main idea
    d. Irrelevant

Answer: b. Too specific. The paragraph discusses the whole concept of pleasure, not just the happiness to be found in a boy-girl relationship.

Memory is a fundamental factor in intelligence. Without it there could hardly be any intelligence. If we did not remember any of the words we heard, the faces we saw, the general information we acquired, the places we have been in, etc., we should be hopeless idiots. We should not remember what food to eat or what clothes to wear, we could learn no lessons, and consequently we should be constantly in a chaotic state.

77. Memory is one of the many aspects of intelligence.
    a. Too general
    b. Too specific
    c. Main idea
    d. Irrelevant

Answer: a. Too general. The paragraph is not concerned with the many aspects of intelligence—only with memory.

78. A photographic memory is an advantage for students.
    a. Too general
    b. Too specific
    c. Main idea
    d. Irrelevant

Answer: d. Irrelevant. The paragraph makes no such claim.

79. A necessary condition of intelligence is memory.
    a. Too general
    b. Too specific
    c. Main idea
    d. Irrelevant

Answer: c. Main idea

80. A man who suffered from amnesia would probably not be very intelligent.
    a. Too general
    b. Too specific
    c. Main idea
    d. Irrelevant

Answer: d. Irrelevant. The paragraph is not concerned with amnesia.

Outstanding performers of music, nearly always, have had special talents since childhood—a beautiful voice, unusual manual dexterity, an excellent ear for pitch, or a keen memory. Like athletes, they have exceptional coordination, strength, and competitive drive. Most pianists and violinists play professionally before the age of ten.

81. Outstanding performers are very gifted and have special talents.
    a. Too general
    b. Too specific
    c. Main idea
    d. Irrelevant

Answer: a. Too general. The paragraph has a more specific point.

82. Most violinists play professionally before the age of ten.
    a. Too general
    b. Too specific
    c. Main idea
    d. Irrelevant

Answer: b. Too specific. The paragraph refers to other performers as well as violinists.

83. Which of the following is irrelevant?
    a. Outstanding performers have special talents when they are very young.
    b. Outstanding performers, like athletes, are very competitive.
    c. Most pianists and violinists play professionally before the age of ten.
    d. Most pianists and violinists have poor singing voices.

Answer: d.

84. Most outstanding performers have had special talents since childhood.
    a. Too general
    b. Too specific
    c. Main idea
    d. Irrelevant

Answer: c. Main idea

Anyone can ask questions. However, good questioning is a high art. To be valuable scientifically, a question must be relevant and it must be testable. The difficulty is that it is often very hard or impossible to tell in advance whether a question is relevant or irrelevant, testable or untestable. If a man collapses on the street and passers-by want to help him, it may or may not be relevant to ask when he had his last meal. Without experience one cannot decide on the relevance of this question, and the wrong procedure might be followed.

85. Journalists must be able to ask good questions.
    a. Too general
    b. Too specific
    c. Main idea
    d. Irrelevant

Answer: d. Irrelevant. There is no mention of journalists in the paragraph.

86. To be valuable scientifically, a question must be relevant and testable.
    a. Too general
    b. Too specific
    c. Main idea
    d. Irrelevant

Answer: c. Main idea

87. It is impossible to tell in advance whether a question is relevant and testable.
    a. Too general
    b. Too specific
    c. Main idea
    d. Irrelevant

Answer: b. Too specific. The paragraph is about the criteria for determining the value of questions. This statement is about one aspect of the criteria.

88. Teachers should be able to ask good questions.
    a. Too general
    b. Too specific
    c. Main idea
    d. Irrelevant

Answer: d. Irrelevant. The paragraph makes no mention of teachers.

The air at high altitudes is rarefied (lesser barometric pressure), and a given volume contains less oxygen than at sea level. This affects the normal respiratory needs of men and animals. A mountain climber or person in an airplane must use a tank of oxygen and a face mask to obtain adequate oxygen. Planes operating above 10,000 ft (3,000 m) usually have the air pressure inside raised (pressurized) to facilitate breathing.

89. At higher altitudes, where the air is rarefied and contains less oxygen, people need extra oxygen or pressurized air to breathe normally.
   a. Too general
   b. Too specific
   c. Main idea
   d. Irrelevant

Answer: c. Main idea

90. Which of the following is too specific?
   a. The air at higher altitudes is usually colder.
   b. Mountain climbers need tanks of oxygen to breathe normally.
   c. The air at higher altitudes is rarefied and contains less oxygen.
   d. Mountain climbers usually have large lung capacities.

Answer: b.

91. The air at higher altitudes is different from the air at sea level.
   a. Too general
   b. Too specific
   c. Main idea
   d. Irrelevant

Answer: a. Too general. The paragraph tells how it is different.

92. The air at higher altitudes is usually colder.
   a. Too general
   b. Too specific
   c. Main idea
   d. Irrelevant

Answer: d. Irrelevant. The paragraph makes no mention of air temperature.

When a message offers to foretell the future, whether it concerns the stock market, an election, or other event in the future, the listener should remind himself that a prediction is only a prediction, and that prophets can be mistaken. . . .

Even when the prediction is based on facts, the strong possibility exists that someone else might have interpreted the same facts differently. All economists, for example, have access to the main facts about unemployment, income, capital expenditures, carloadings, and the various indexes; but at a given moment one economist may feel that the country is headed for further recession, a second that it has hit the bottom of the recession, and a third that it is beginning to head upward out of the recession.

93. Stock market predictions can be wrong.
    a. Too general
    b. Too specific
    c. Main idea
    d. Irrelevant

Answer: b. Too specific. The paragraph refers to all kinds of predictions.

94. Astrologers usually make very general predictions.
    a. Too general
    b. Too specific
    c. Main idea
    d. Irrelevant

Answer: d. Irrelevant. There is no mention of astrologers in the paragraph.

95. Which of the following is the main idea?
    a. The stock market may go either up or down.
    b. Most predictions are not as good as we think they are.
    c. Listeners should remember that predictions may or may not come
       true.
    d. Some economists feel that the country is headed for further recession.

Answer: c.

96. Listeners should be critical of things they hear and not accept them blindly.
    a. Too general
    b. Too specific
    c. Main idea
    d. Irrelevant

Answer: a. Too general. The paragraph suggests that listeners should be critical
of predictions.

Progress Check Number One

Review

Referring now to your tally card, add all your errors for *each* of the four categories. If you made more than five errors in any of the categories, you should review the page indicated for that category:

	Page	Frame Number
Main idea	2	1–4
Too general	4	5–8
Too specific	6	9–12
Irrelevant	8	13–16

Total

After you have summed your errors for the individual categories and reviewed, if necessary, you should add the total number of errors for all four categories. If your total number of errors is less than twenty, see alternative 1 below. If more than twenty, see alternative 2.

Alternatives

1. If you made fewer than twenty errors, skip to Part 4, page 77, and continue the exercises from there.
2. If you made more than twenty errors, you need more practice and should continue through Part 3 starting on page 55. Keep track of your errors on the answer sheet. As soon as you have completed ten consecutive answers without making an error, you may skip to Part 4, page 77, and continue with the exercises from there.

Part 3:
More Practice Recognizing the Main Idea

Religion was a far more important part of life to colonial America than it is today. It was something without which a way of life simply could not be conceived. The weekly sermon and the theological tract were in many places the entire diet of the mind. The great majority of all printed books were religious. We cannot picture New England without the congregations, or Pennsylvania without Quaker meetinghouses, or even the Virginia gentleman without his Episcopal church. And after 1740 we can scarcely think of the frontier without the revival or the camp meeting.

97. Religion has had an important role in America.
    a. Too general
    b. Too specific
    c. Main idea
    d. Irrelevant

Answer: a. Too general. The paragraph discusses religion in colonial America.

98. Most printed books in colonial times were religious.
    a. Too general
    b. Too specific
    c. Main idea
    d. Irrelevant

Answer: b. Too specific. Religious books are only one example of the importance of religion in colonial life.

99. One cannot conceive of the colonial way of life without religion's playing an important role.
    a. Too general
    b. Too specific
    c. Main idea
    d. Irrelevant

Answer: c. Main idea

100. Colonial children were required to memorize catechism questions.
    a. Too general
    b. Too specific
    c. Main idea
    d. Irrelevant

Answer: d. Irrelevant. The catechism is not mentioned.

While it is possible to find in the plant kingdom as a whole all shades and combinations of the colors of the spectrum, there is in general a predominance of the primary colors: green, yellow, red, and blue. These colors are imparted to the plant by definite chemical compounds, or pigments, each of which has its own characteristic color. The particular color which a plant assumes is usually caused by the predominance of one or another of these pigments in a combination of several of them. When plant parts appear white, it is because of the absence of pigments. Sunlight falling on such parts is transmitted or reflected practically as received, and hence such parts appear white or colorless. The opaqueness of this white is intensified by the refractive powers of cell walls and often by the presence of air spaces in the tissues.

101. In the plant kingdom there is a general predominance of the primary colors.
   a. Too general
   b. Too specific
   c. Main idea
   d. Irrelevant

Answer: b. Too specific. The paragraph is more concerned with the factors determining the colors of plants.

102. All the colors in the spectrum can be formed by combinations of the primary colors.
   a. Too general
   b. Too specific
   c. Main idea
   d. Irrelevant

Answer: d. Irrelevant. This fact is not mentioned in the paragraph.

103. If a plant or portion of a plant contains no pigment then it appears white.
   a. Too general
   b. Too specific
   c. Main idea
   d. Irrelevant

Answer: b. Too specific. This summary takes into consideration only part of the paragraph.

104. The refractive powers of cell walls tend to intensify the white reflected in plant parts.
   a. Too general
   b. Too specific
   c. Main idea
   d. Irrelevant

Answer: b. Too specific. This statement mentions only an isolated fact about plant colors.

The substance of the universe, the earth, and living organisms is termed matter. Under different environmental conditions of temperature and pressure, any particular kind of matter may be in one of three physical states—solid, liquid, or gas. Water, a common type of matter, may be variously solid ice, fluid water, or water vapor. Animal shells and skeletons are mostly of solids, the blood plasma and much of the content of body cells are fluid, and gasses are present in lungs or dissolved in body fluids. Almost any animal comprises matter in three states.

105. All substances may exist as either solids, liquids, or gases.
  a. Too general
  b. Too specific
  c. Main idea
  d. Irrelevant

Answer: c. Main idea

106. Much practical use is made of the laws that govern the states of matter.
  a. Too general
  b. Too specific
  c. Main idea
  d. Irrelevant

Answer: d. Irrelevant. The paragraph is not concerned with "practical use."

107. As matter experiences pressure and temperature changes, it varies from a solid to a liquid to a gaseous state.
  a. Too general
  b. Too specific
  c. Main idea
  d. Irrelevant

Answer: b. Too specific. This statement elaborates on the relationship of states of matter.

108. Water, depending on the temperature, can exist as a solid, liquid, or gas.
  a. Too general
  b. Too specific
  c. Main idea
  d. Irrelevant

Answer: b. Too specific. This is only an example.

Perhaps the oldest of all theories of state origin in political science is the idea that God ordained and established it. This notion prevailed in the ancient Oriental empires, where the rulers themselves were regarded as the descendants of gods. The early Hebrews thought that the Lord had created their governmental order, and the early Christians believed that God had imposed the state upon man as a punishment for his sins, as signalized by Adam's fall from the grace of God in the Garden of Eden. Centuries later, Thomas Paine, the pamphleteer of the American Revolution, expressed much the same idea when he declared: "Government, like dress, is the badge of lost innocence."

109. There are several theories which explain the origin of the state.
  a. Too general
  b. Too specific
  c. Main idea
  d. Irrelevant

Answer: a. Too general. The paragraph specifically describes the theory of divine establishment of the state.

110. The notion of divine establishment of the state prevailed in the ancient Orient.
  a. Too general
  b. Too specific
  c. Main idea
  d. Irrelevant

Answer: b. Too specific. This is a specific example of the ancient concept of divine establishment of the state.

111. One of the oldest theories of the origin of the state is that the state was established by God.
  a. Too general
  b. Too specific
  c. Main idea
  d. Irrelevant

Answer: c. Main idea

112. Thomas Paine was the first person to realize the significance of the divine-establishment theory to political science.
  a. Too general
  b. Too specific
  c. Main idea
  d. Irrelevant

Answer: d. Irrelevant. There is no mention in the paragraph of any significance recognized by Paine.

One can hardly touch on the process of inheritance without raising the question of improving the quality of people genetically, that is, through selective mating. Would the average quality of our people be raised if the more gifted had more offspring and the dull and feeble-minded had very few, if any? Most of our inadequates are born not of parents who are idiots or imbeciles, but of parents at the moron or borderline level. Even though parents of low intelligence and character did not have offspring, however, incompetents would still be born to capable parents, for the germ cells of some of them contain defective genes. Nevertheless, there would be fewer defectives, and they would become progressively fewer from generation to generation. People would carry fewer and fewer determiners for deficiency.

113. Retarded children sometimes develop emotional and psychological problems.
    a. Too general
    b. Too specific
    c. Main idea
    d. Irrelevant

Answer: d. Irrelevant. The paragraph does not mention emotional problems.

114. The Germans in World War II had a basically sound plan for creating a superior race.
    a. Too general
    b. Too specific
    c. Main idea
    d. Irrelevant

Answer: d. Irrelevant. The paragraph does not concern itself with Germany's plans.

115. A process of selective breeding would genetically improve the overall quality of human beings.
    a. Too general
    b. Too specific
    c. Main idea
    d. Irrelevant

Answer: c. Main idea

116. Genetic selection affects the process of inheritance.
    a. Too general
    b. Too specific
    c. Main idea
    d. Irrelevant

Answer: a. Too general. The paragraph is more concerned with the explanation of genetic characteristics

All the energy used by organisms is derived from the sun. Energy may be transformed from one type to another, but it is never created or destroyed. Plants absorb the radiant energy in sunlight and . . . produce carbohydrates from carbon dioxide and water; they also synthesize proteins and fats. The energy stored in these compounds is the ultimate source used by all animals. Energy relations underlie all physical and biotic processes on the earth and determine the activities of organisms.

117. All organisms depend on the sun.
    a. Too general
    b. Too specific
    c. Main idea
    d. Irrelevant

Answer: a. Too general. The paragraph is specifically concerned with the *energy* derived from the sun.

118. Energy derived from the sun is stored in compounds.
    a. Too general
    b. Too specific
    c. Main idea
    d. Irrelevant

Answer: b. Too specific. This is only a summary of one of the supporting sentences in the paragraph.

119. All energy used by organisms is derived from the sun.
    a. Too general
    b. Too specific
    c. Main idea
    d. Irrelevant

Answer: c. Main idea

120. Special characteristics of energy enable it to be available for organisms to consume.
    a. Too general
    b. Too specific
    c. Main idea
    d. Irrelevant

Answer: d. Irrelevant. The paragraph is not concerned with any "special characteristics" of energy.

The writer must be on his guard against certain common errors which are sometimes made in the framing of a logical definition. A definition should ordinarily avoid being circular, that is, the defining part should not include the term being defined. No real boundaries are established when a Puritan is defined as a believer in Puritanism.

121. Errors should be avoided when framing a logical definition.
    a. Too general
    b. Too specific
    c. Main idea
    d. Irrelevant

Answer: a. Too general. This statement does not discuss circular definitions, as the paragraph does.

122. Writers should avoid using circular definitions in which the defining part contains the term defined.
    a. Too general
    b. Too specific
    c. Main idea
    d. Irrelevant

Answer: c. Main idea

123. Circular definitions are often found in the great works of the earlier philosophers.
    a. Too general
    b. Too specific
    c. Main idea
    d. Irrelevant

Answer: d. Irrelevant. The relationship between circular definitions and early philosophers is not discussed in the paragraph.

124. Defining a Puritan as one who believes in Puritanism is a circular definition.
    a. Too general
    b. Too specific
    c. Main idea
    d. Irrelevant

Answer: b. Too specific. This is only one example of a circular definition.

Political science is the study of the changing, fluid present, rather than of the settled—if often obscure—past. Because of this vital, dynamic character of political science, it is natural that emphasis has shifted, and will continue to shift, from one aspect or specialty to another. Such changes in emphasis are related to new methods of research and to world happenings and problems.

125. Political science is the study of the theory, organization, government, and practice of the state.
   a. Too general
   b. Too specific
   c. Main idea
   d. Irrelevant

Answer: d. Irrelevant. There is no mention of these things in the paragraph.

126. The focus of political science shifts according to developments in research and changes in world events and problems.
   a. Too general
   b. Too specific
   c. Main idea
   d. Irrelevant

Answer: c. Main idea

127. Political science is the study of the changing present, rather than the settled past, thus, its emphasis is always changing.
   a. Too general
   b. Too specific
   c. Main idea
   d. Irrelevant

Answer: c. Main idea

128. Political science is a study which changes its emphasis.
   a. Too general
   b. Too specific
   c. Main idea
   d. Irrelevant

Answer: a. Too general. This statement does not mention the reasons for change.

It is as hard to carry ideas in your mind without a plan as it is to carry an armful of groceries without a basket. Even an experienced speaker would get rattled if he tried to proceed without organization. Let us say that, early in the year, you want to tell us that the school team is certain to have a good season. Instead of merely rambling along, prepare a little outline. Talk first about the team's *offense*, offering examples; talk second about the team's *defense*, with other examples. Such a plan has a steadying effect.

129. In talking about a school team one should first talk about the team's offense.
    a. Too general
    b. Too specific
    c. Main idea
    d. Irrelevant

Answer: b. Too specific. This is only an example.

130. The best defense is a good offense.
    a. Too general
    b. Too specific
    c. Main idea
    d. Irrelevant

Answer: d. Irrelevant. The paragraph is not about sports.

131. Organization and outlining are essential for speaking and have a steadying effect on a speaker.
    a. Too general
    b. Too specific
    c. Main idea
    d. Irrelevant

Answer: c. Main idea

132. Which of the following is irrelevant?
    a. It is hard to carry ideas in your mind without a plan.
    b. Organization is very important in public speaking.
    c. Even experienced speakers need to organize.
    d. Many speakers get rattled when they talk about sports.

Answer: d.

Temperature influences the growth, fruiting, and survival of the plants upon which various animals depend for food. A prolonged cold spring delays the development of grasses and leaves upon which many insects, rodents, and grazing animals forage and may determine their survival. Unseasonable weather at blossoming time may reduce the subsequent crops of berries or seeds on which various birds feed, forcing them to wander elsewhere for food or starve.

133. A good crop for the farmers means plenty of food for the field mice.
    a. Too general
    b. Too specific
    c. Main idea
    d. Irrelevant

Answer: d. Irrelevant. There is no mention of the relationship of a good crop for the farmers to the food supply of field mice.

134. Temperature may determine the survival of plants and the animals that depend on them.
    a. Too general
    b. Too specific
    c. Main idea
    d. Irrelevant

Answer: c. Main idea

135. Boysenberries are especially good food for small rodents.
    a. Too general
    b. Too specific
    c. Main idea
    d. Irrelevant

Answer: d. Irrelevant. No mention is made of any particular berry.

136. Birds are dependent upon seasonable weather for survival.
    a. Too general
    b. Too specific
    c. Main idea
    d. Irrelevant

Answer: b. Too specific. Other animals besides birds are dependent upon the temperature.

Part 4:
Working with the Main Idea

You will now be doing more exercises of the same type, but with somewhat more difficult material. You will need another answer sheet just like the first one. Keep a record of your errors by circling the corresponding number on the card. *You do not have to keep track of the kind of error—just the number of errors.*

A *special-purpose* computer, as the name implies, is designed to perform one specific task. The program of instructions is built into the machine. Specialization results in the given task being performed economically, quickly, and efficiently. A disadvantage, however, is that the machine lacks versatility; it is inflexible and cannot be used to perform other operations. Special-purpose computers designed for the sole purpose of solving complex navigational problems are installed in our atomic submarines but could not be used for other purposes unless their circuits were redesigned.

137. Special-purpose computers solve navigational problems in atomic submarines.
    a. Too general
    b. Too specific
    c. Main idea
    d. Irrelevant

Answer: b. Too specific. This is only an example.

138. Which of the following is irrelevant?
    a. A special-purpose computer is designed to perform a specific task.
    b. Special-purpose computers are not very flexible.
    c. Special-purpose computers are economical and efficient.
    d. Special-purpose computers are very expensive.

Answer: d.

139. Special-purpose computers are designed for a specific task. They are efficient and economical but lack flexibility.
    a. Too general
    b. Too specific
    c. Main idea
    d. Irrelevant

Answer: c. Main idea

140. General-purpose computers are not very flexible.
    a. Too general
    b. Too specific
    c. Main idea
    d. Irrelevant

Answer: d. Irrelevant. The paragraph does not mention general-purpose computers.

A problem of the modern legislature is the question of its proper size. In general, large assemblies are criticized as unwieldy and inefficient; they are forced to work largely through committees or to delegate much authority to a cabinet or president or to various administrative bodies. Yet there seems little disposition to reduce the size of national legislatures; the House of Commons numbers 630 members; the House of Lords, about 800; the new National Assembly of France, 626; the United States House of Representatives, 435. To reduce the size of the legislative body would necessitate enlarging the district and thus the number of voters represented by the legislator. Constituencies are already so large and populous as to impair if not destroy the personal relationship between the voter and his representative.

141. Smaller legislatures or assemblies will result in a modernized state.
    a. Too general
    b. Too specific
    c. Main idea
    d. Irrelevant

Answer: d. Irrelevant. There is no mention of this in the paragraph.

142. A primary problem in legislatures is size: Large units are cumbersome, and small units are less representative.
    a. Too general
    b. Too specific
    c. Main idea
    d. Irrelevant

Answer: c. Main idea

143. All men have the right to life, liberty, and the pursuit of happiness.
    a. Too general
    b. Too specific
    c. Main idea
    d. Irrelevant

Answer: d. Irrelevant. There is no mention of this right in the paragraph.

144. In order to reduce the size of the legislative body, voting districts would have to be enlarged.
    a. Too general
    b. Too specific
    c. Main idea
    d. Irrelevant

Answer: b. Too specific. This statement discusses only one part of the problem of large legislatures.

Heuristic is a word that means *serving to discover.* It is used to describe the judgmental, or *common sense*, part of problem solving. That is, it describes that part of problem solving which deals with the definition of the problem, the selection of reasonable strategies to be followed (which may or may not lead to optimum solutions), and the formulation of hypotheses and hunches. Human beings are *far superior* to the computer in the heuristic area of intellectual work.

145. Which of the following is too specific?
    a. Computers operate much faster than people.
    b. *Heuristic* means *serving to discover.*
    c. Human beings are far superior to computers in every possible way.
    d. Computers have no "common sense."

Answer: *b.*

146. Human beings are better than computers at some tasks.
    a. Too general
    b. Too specific
    c. Main idea
    d. Irrelevant

Answer: *a.* Too general. The paragraph specifies which tasks people perform better than computers.

147. Human beings are far superior to computers in the heuristic, or common sense, part of problem solving.
    a. Too general
    b. Too specific
    c. Main idea
    d. Irrelevant

Answer: *c.* Main idea

148. Digital computers are very heuristic.
    a. Too general
    b. Too specific
    c. Main idea
    d. Irrelevant

Answer: *d.* Irrelevant. The paragraph does not mention digital computers.

A common practice of students is to pass over tables, charts, and formulas. These are included to summarize in effective form the data pertinent to the discussion. Often they require careful study and consequently are skipped. A good plan is to study tables, charts, and formulas until every detail is clearly comprehended and a conclusion drawn. In the case of the formulas particularly, it may be necessary to memorize them, but the meaning of the symbols should be understood before they are memorized, for memorizing meaningful material is more effective than memorizing material the meaning of which is not comprehended.

149. Tables and charts require careful study in order to be understood.
    a. Too general
    b. Too specific
    c. Main idea
    d. Irrelevant

Answer: b. Too specific. This statement mentions only one fact about tables and charts.

150. Formulas should be memorized exactly.
    a. Too general
    b. Too specific
    c. Main idea
    d. Irrelevant

Answer: b. Too specific. This statement refers to only one example given in the paragraph.

151. Studying tables and formulas can lead to a better understanding of mathematics.
    a. Too general
    b. Too specific
    c. Main idea
    d. Irrelevant
Answer: d. Irrelevant. There is no mention of the relationship of studying tables and formulas to understanding mathematics in the paragraph.

152. Tables, charts, and formulas can be extremely beneficial to the conscientious student if they are studied and understood.
    a. Too general
    b. Too specific
    c. Main idea
    d. Irrelevant

Answer: c. Main idea

Another device intended to safeguard liberty was the separation of powers. The new state constitutions usually provided for separate executive, legislative, and judicial departments, each clothed with its own authority and able to carry on its functions independently of the others. The purpose was to throw obstacles in the way of a seizure of power. An individual or a faction, though supreme in one branch, could not legally override the others and bring all parts of the government under single unified control.

153. A safeguard of liberty in state constitutions is the separation of powers to prevent seizure of control by an individual or a faction.
    a. Too general
    b. Too specific
    c. Main idea
    d. Irrelevant

Answer: c. Main idea

154. The state constitutions provide for separate executive, legislative, and judicial departments.
    a. Too general
    b. Too specific
    c. Main idea
    d. Irrelevant
Answer: b. Too specific. This statement deals only with the method of separating powers.

155. The writers of the state constitutions were fearful of the seizure of power by an individual or a faction.
    a. Too general
    b. Too specific
    c. Main idea
    d. Irrelevant
Answer: d. Irrelevant. There is no statement in the paragraph about the attitudes of the writers of state constitutions.

156. The state constitutions provided for safeguards of liberty.
    a. Too general
    b. Too specific
    c. Main idea
    d. Irrelevant

Answer: a. Too general. The paragraph deals specifically with the separation of powers as a safeguard.

Elvis Presley [1935–1977] caught the essence of the early rock 'n' roll sexual revolution. On stage, there was no doubt about the focus of attention. He offered sex appeal. While his view of women was hardly liberated, "You Ain't Nothin' But a Hound Dog" kept women swooning. "Love Me Tender" offered a softer, warmer, almost affectionate side that contrasted with his blatant sexuality.

157. The song "You Ain't Nothin' But a Hound Dog" kept women swooning.
    a. Too general
    b. Too specific
    c. Main idea
    d. Irrelevant

Answer: *b.* Too specific. The paragraph is mainly about Elvis, not the song.

158. Which of the following is irrelevant?
    a. Elvis was a well-known rock'n'roll star.
    b. Elvis offered sex appeal to his audiences.
    c. On stage, Elvis was the focus of attention.
    d. Elvis was seldom seen in public except at his concerts.

Answer: *d.*

159. Elvis had a powerful effect on his audiences because he caught the essence of the rock'n'roll sexual revolution.
    a. Too general
    b. Too specific
    c. Main idea
    d. Irrelevant

Answer: *c.* Main idea

160. Elvis was a very popular performer.
    a. Too general
    b. Too specific
    c. Main idea
    d. Irrelevant

Answer: *a.* Too general. The paragraph explains why Elvis was popular.

Economic scarcity refers to the basic fact of life that there exists only a finite amount of human and nonhuman resources, which the best technical knowledge is capable of using to produce only a limited maximum amount of each and every good. And thus far, nowhere on the globe is the supply of goods so plentiful or the tastes of the populace so limited that every person can have more than enough of everything he might fancy.

161. Economic scarcity means that there is a limited maximum amount of goods available in the world.
    a. Too general
    b. Too specific
    c. Main idea
    d. Irrelevant

Answer: c. Main idea

---

162. Nowhere in the world is the supply of goods so plentiful that everyone can have everything he or she wants.
    a. Too general
    b. Too specific
    c. Main idea
    d. Irrelevant

Answer: b. Too specific. This statement does not include a definition of economic scarcity.

---

163. The world is in danger of not producing enough goods to satisfy consumer demands.
    a. Too general
    b. Too specific
    c. Main idea
    d. Irrelevant

Answer: d. Irrelevant. There is no mention of a world danger in the paragraph.

---

164. Economic scarcity refers to the fact that there is no way to make all goods available in unlimited quantity.
    a. Too general
    b. Too specific
    c. Main idea
    d. Irrelevant

Answer: c. Main idea

Ethics are concerned with individual morality. They involve motive as well as action, for the area of ethics suggests that motive, no less than action, affects the character of the individual. Ethics encompass rules which describe basic goodness and rightness. They embody the absolute ideal upon which man should pattern his conduct. Voluntary adherence by the individual to such ideal rules, it is assumed, will necessarily promote the good life.

165. Ethics may be distinguished from laws.
    a. Too general
    b. Too specific
    c. Main idea
    d. Irrelevant

Answer: *d.* Irrelevant. There is no mention of the difference between ethics and laws in this paragraph.

166. Ethics is a branch of philosophy.
    a. Too general
    b. Too specific
    c. Main idea
    d. Irrelevant

Answer: *d.* Irrelevant. No mention is made of the relationship between ethics and philosophy.

167. It is assumed that voluntary adherence to a code of ethics will help promote a good life.
    a. Too general
    b. Too specific
    c. Main idea
    d. Irrelevant

Answer: *b.* Too specific. This summarizes only a small part of the meaning of ethics as explained in the paragraph.

168. Ethics include rules which describe basic goodness and rightness as well as an ideal pattern of conduct.
    a. Too general
    b. Too specific
    c. Main idea
    d. Irrelevant

Answer: *c.* Main idea

The artist of the Paleolithic period apparently did not distinguish between the image he created on the walls of the caves and the reality or fact that was pictured. To him the image was reality, not a symbol or spiritual essence, as it would be later to artists of the Neolithic Age. Therefore the bulk of Paleolithic art is naturalistic in form and meaning, trying to bring the image into concurrence with the object portrayed, to create an identity that would help obtain the desired object.

169. The Paleolithic artist did not distinguish between image and reality and used art, which was consequently naturalistic in form, as an identity that would help obtain the desired object.
    a. Too general
    b. Too specific
    c. Main idea
    d. Irrelevant

Answer: c. Main idea

170. Paleolithic artists, as a rule, were poorer artists than those of the Neolithic Age.
    a. Too general
    b. Too specific
    c. Main idea
    d. Irrelevant

Answer: d. Irrelevant. The paragraph makes no mention of the relative artistic merit of Paleolithic and Neolithic artists.

171. Most Paleolithic art is naturalistic.
    a. Too general
    b. Too specific
    c. Main idea
    d. Irrelevant

Answer: a. Too general. The paragraph explains why most Paleolithic art was done naturalistically.

172. Paleolithic art was naturalistic in form because the artist did not distinguish image from reality and used art to help obtain a desired object.
    a. Too general
    b. Too specific
    c. Main idea
    d. Irrelevant

Answer: c. Main idea

No nation is free from the threat of epidemics when diseases are permitted to run rampant in other countries. Modern transportation has many advantages, but it also provides for the rapid movement of insect vectors, as well as human carriers, of many communicable diseases. Breakfast in England, lunch in North America, and back to England for tea is now possible. Even greater speeds are forecast as "jet," "rocket," and "atomic" become commonplace adjectives in a discussion of transportation and as man extends his explorations of space. Such rapid movement adds immeasurably to the problem of controlling the spread of communicable diseases.

173. A European epidemic of typhus could be brought to the United States.
      a. Too general
      b. Too specific
      c. Main idea
      d. Irrelevant

Answer: *d.* Irrelevant. No mention of specific diseases is made in the paragraph.

174. Drugs to contain the spread of disease are easily available in today's jet age.
      a. Too general
      b. Too specific
      c. Main idea
      d. Irrelevant

Answer: *d.* Irrelevant. The paragraph is not concerned with drugs.

175. Modern transportation provides rapid movement of insect vectors.
      a. Too general
      b. Too specific
      c. Main idea
      d. Irrelevant

Answer: *b.* Too specific. The paragraph is also concerned with human carriers.

176. Modern transportation makes the problem of communicable disease control harder to solve because diseases can travel more rapidly.
      a. Too general
      b. Too specific
      c. Main idea
      d. Irrelevant

Answer: *c.* Main idea

Progress Check Number Two

Review
Referring to your tally card, add up your errors for this part. If you made more than ten errors, you should review pages 2 to 9.

Total
If your total number of errors is less than ten see alternative 1 below.
If more than ten, see alternative 2.

Alternatives
1. If you made fewer than ten errors, skip Part 5 and turn to page 133 and continue the exercises from there.
2. If your total number of errors is more than ten, you should work through Part 5, starting on page 101. As soon as you have completed ten consecutive exercises without making a single error, you may skip to Part 6 on page 133.

Progress Check Number Two

Part 5:
More Practice Working with the Main Idea

Virtually all the mathematics had its roots somewhere in nature. Arithmetic and algebra grew out of men's needs for counting, financial management, and other simple operations of daily life; geometry and trigonometry developed from problems of land measurement, surveying, and astronomy; and calculus was invented to assist in the solution of certain basic problems in physics. In recent years new forms of mathematics have been invented to help us cope with problems in social science, business, biology, and warfare; and new mathematical subjects are sure to arise from other portions of human endeavor.

177. Calculus was invented to help in solving problems in physics.
   a. Too general
   b. Too specific
   c. Main idea
   d. Irrelevant

Answer: *b.* Too specific. In this paragraph calculus is used only as an example of one use of mathematics.

178. Mathematics is a difficult, although rewarding, subject.
   The above summary is *irrelevant* because:
   a. The paragraph makes no mention of the difficulty of mathematics.
   b. The paragraph is not at all concerned with the practical aspects of mathematics.
   c. Everyone knows without being told that mathematics is difficult.
   d. The paragraph is concerned with the origins rather than with the processes of mathematics.

Answer: *a.*

179. Most of the disciplines of mathematics have arisen to enable man to cope with problems in nature.
   a. Too general
   b. Too specific
   c. Main idea
   d. Irrelevant

Answer: *c.* Main idea

180. Mathematics has clarified many laws of physical science.
   a. Too general
   b. Too specific
   c. Main idea
   d. Irrelevant

Answer: *b.* Too specific. Physical science is only one area of nature that encouraged the application of mathematics.

Much of personality is shaped by social patterns. In the traditions of family, church, and nation, certain situations are defined as pleasant, unpleasant, exciting, or depressing. The differences between the "volatile Latin" and the "phlegmatic Briton" are chiefly matters of cultural expectation. In a family with a military tradition, admission to West Point might be a very pleasurable experience—failure, a cause for depression. The playing of social roles—e.g., as girl or as boy—is to a considerable extent a matter of adopting the culturally defined view of proper feelings and behavior. Children growing up in a "smart-set" family acquire patterns of feeling, perception, and behavior different from those of a working-class family.

181. Differences between the "volatile Latin" and the "phlegmatic Briton" are caused mainly by differing cultural expectations.
    a. Too general
    b. Too specific
    c. Main idea
    d. Irrelevant

Answer: b. Too specific. This statement mentions an example of the effects of differing social patterns.

182. According to the paragraph, if a boy's father was a military man, that boy would experience social pressures upon him to follow in his father's footsteps.
    a. Too general
    b. Too specific
    c. Main idea
    d. Irrelevant

Answer: b. Too specific. This makes mention of only one idea in the paragraph.

183. **Which of the following is the best summary of the paragraph?**
    a. Social patterns and pressures have much to do with the shaping of an individual's behavior.
    b. Individual differences are merely a matter of differing social patterns.
    c. Children from "smart-set" families are different from those from working-class families.
    d. Conformity is almost always a function of family or "in-group" pressures.

Answer: a.

184. The behavior of a boy brought up in a stable environment would perhaps be more socially acceptable than would the behavior of a boy from a "broken home."
    a. Too general
    b. Too specific
    c. Main idea
    d. Irrelevant

Answer: d. Irrelevant. The paragraph is not concerned with social acceptance.

Dylan had nothing musical to offer the Beatles. But lyrics are the essence of folk music, and Dylan could write lyrics. Like the Rolling Stones, he was angry; but, far from being detached, he wrote songs about human feelings. "Blowin' in the Wind," "It's a Hard Rain," and "It's All Right, Ma," are antiwar songs dealing with oppression, atomic holocaust, senseless killing, and wasted human life. Dylan was personal, something pop music had never quite been before. Lennon and McCartney (the main Beatle songwriters) were affected. "Yesterday" is their lament about the difficulties of love between people.

185. Bob Dylan was heavily influenced by the Beatles.
   a. Too general
   b. Too specific
   c. Main idea
   d. Irrelevant

Answer: d. Irrelevant. No mention is made in the paragraph of the Beatles influencing Dylan.

186. The Beatles were influenced by Bob Dylan, who wrote excellent lyrics, and pop music became personal for the first time.
   a. Too general
   b. Too specific
   c. Main idea
   d. Irrelevant

Answer: c. Main idea

187. Lyrics are the essence of folk music.
   a. Too general
   b. Too specific
   c. Main idea
   d. Irrelevant

Answer: b. Too specific. The paragraph is mainly about the Beatles being influenced by Dylan.

188. Which of the following is too specific?
   a. Bob Dylan was not very good at writing lyrics.
   b. Bob Dylan and the Beatles never met.
   c. Dylan wrote songs about human feelings.
   d. The Beatles were very popular.

Answer: c.

Although classification and division is one of the more sophisticated methods of analysis, it is used at some time or another by everyone. A favorite indoor sport of Americans has come to be applying labels to the rest of the population. We speak glibly in these middle years of the twentieth century of the "organization man," the "man in the gray flannel suit," the suburbanite, the exurbanite, and the Ivy Leaguer. What we are really doing is classifying certain people, putting them into a category suggested by the characteristics that they possess. In a well-known essay Russell Lynes classified Americans, according to their tastes, as high-brow, middle-brow, and low-brow. An economist might classify Americans, according to their economic standing, as low-income group, middle-income group, and high-income group. In all these cases, certain characteristics have been classified, assigned to a category.

189. Certain prominent Americans tend to classify people according to
their tastes or economic standing.
   a. Too general
   b. Too specific
   c. Main idea
   d. Irrelevant

Answer: *b.* Too specific. The paragraph refers to everyone's classifying
others—not just a particular group.

190. Classification of people is an asset to the American way of life.
   a. Too general
   b. Too specific
   c. Main idea
   d. Irrelevant

Answer: *d.* Irrelevant. Whether or not classification of people is good is
not mentioned in the paragraph.

191. Which of the following is the main idea?
   a. Labeling is a favorite American indoor sport.
   b. Classification and division is one of the more sophisticated
       methods of analysis.
   c. Classifications differ depending upon the purpose for the
       classification.
   d. It is characteristic of Americans to classify people into various
       categories according to social or economic characteristics.

Answer: *d.*

192. The purpose of classifying people is to understand them better.
   a. Too general
   b. Too specific
   c. Main idea
   d. Irrelevant

Answer: *d.* Irrelevant. There is no mention in the paragraph of the
purpose of classification of people.

For long ages, tribal magic was the rallying point of society, the central institution in which were concentrated the accumulated wisdom and experiences of the day. The execution of magical procedures was in the hands of specially trained individuals, the medicine men and their equivalents. These were the forerunners of the scientists and the clergymen of today.

193. Tribal magic had an important role in society for many ages.
    a. Too general
    b. Too specific
    c. Main idea
    d. Irrelevant

Answer: b. Too general. This statement is vague concerning the specific functions of magic described in the paragraph.

194. Which of the following is irrelevant?
    a. Tribal magic was executed by specially trained individuals.
    b. Tribal magic was the central social institution.
    c. Tribal magic, even today, remains an important institution in many areas.
    d. The accumulated wisdom and experience of the day were concentrated in tribal magic.
Answer: c.

195. Tribal magic was a central institution of wisdom and experience whose magical procedures were executed by specially trained individuals.
    a. Too general
    b. Too specific
    c. Main idea
    d. Irrelevant
Answer: c. Main idea

196. The trained individuals who executed the magical procedures of tribal magic were the forerunners of modern-day scientists.
    a. Too general
    b. Too specific
    c. Main idea
    d. Irrelevant
Answer: b. Too specific. The paragraph deals mainly with the function of tribal magic. This statement is derived from additional information supplied by the paragraph.

The crowning achievement of Jefferson's first administration was the purchase of Louisiana in 1803. In doubling the area of the United States, Jefferson provided an ample estate upon which his dream of an American agrarian democracy might be realized. He wished his country to remain, if possible, a land of small independent farmers. If land ever became scarce, the opportunity for future generations to remain economically independent might disappear. The purchase of Louisiana could postpone that day, Jefferson thought, for a thousand years.

197. Which of the following is too specific?
   a. The purchase of the Louisiana Territory had a tremendous effect on America's future.
   b. Jefferson thought that no more land would be purchased for a thousand years.
   c. Jefferson authorized the purchase of the Louisiana Territory because land was becoming scarce.
   d. Jefferson himself owned a rural estate named Monticello.

Answer: b.

198. Napoleon was eager to sell the Louisiana Territory to the United States because of the financial and political problems caused by his Continental wars.
   a. Too general
   b. Too specific
   c. Main idea
   d. Irrelevant
Answer: d. Irrelevant. This statement has nothing to do with Jefferson's dream of an agrarian democracy.

199. Jefferson doubled the area of the United States by the Louisiana Purchase of 1803.
   a. Too general
   b. Too specific
   c. Main idea
   d. Irrelevant
Answer: b. Too specific. This statement ignores the rest of the paragraph which deals with the reasons and effects of the purchase.

200. Jefferson hoped to realize his dream of an agrarian democracy by doubling the area of the United States by the Louisiana Purchase of 1803.
   a. Too general
   b. Too specific
   c. Main idea
   d. Irrelevant
Answer: c. Main idea

Although the question has long since become purely academic, it is interesting to ask whether our Constitution was itself "constitutional" in the manner of its adoption. Delegates without authority to do more than amend the Articles of Confederation, and representing only twelve of the thirteen states, had brought forth a proposed new constitution. Amendments to the Articles required ratification by all the states before becoming effective. The Constitution was proclaimed as in effect after the ninth state had ratified; thus, at this point—and despite later additional ratifications—it was an unconstitutional constitution. Some writers have described the Constitutional Convention as marking the second American revolution; others have termed it a coup d'état engineered by conservative interests.

201. The Constitution was ratified by only nine of the thirteen original
states.
    a. Too general
    b. Too specific
    c. Main idea
    d. Irrelevant

Answer: b. Too specific. This is only one of the reasons why the adoption
of the Constitution could be considered unconstitutional.

202. Which of the following is irrelevant?
    a. Amendments to the Articles required ratification by all the states
       before becoming effective.
    b. The Constitution provides the basis for democracy.
    c. The Constitution at the time it became effective had received
       ratification from only nine states.
    d. The delegates who adopted the Constitution actually had
       authority only to amend the Articles of Confederation.

Answer: b.

203. Some commentators feel the Constitutional Convention was
engineered by conservative interests.
    a. Too general
    b. Too specific
    c. Main idea
    d. Irrelevant
Answer: b. Too specific. This statement ignores the question of the
Constitution's unconstitutionality.

204. According to the paragraph, the adoption of the Constitution was,
in itself, an unconstitutional act.
    a. Too general
    b. Too specific
    c. Main idea
    d. Irrelevant

Answer: c. Main idea

It is proper to state that personalities differ on specific traits and that such traits can be identified by such pairs of polarized terms as sociable-seclusive, impulsive-inhibited, excited-calm, and the like. It would, however, be misleading to leave the discussion at this point, suggesting that personalities can be sharply divided into these dichotomized classifications. Just as we do not classify rates of flow of water into two groups, fast and slow, but resort to numerical measures of speed, so can we use numerical estimates of the extent to which these trait names are characteristic of an individual.

205. The labeling of personality traits of an individual enables an observer to predict the behavior of the individual.

The above is irrelevant because:

    a. The paragraph has nothing to do with personality traits.

    b. The paragraph is primarily concerned with individual differences.

    c. No mention is made of predictable behavior in this paragraph.

    d. The paragraph is concerned only with normative behavior and does not mention individual traits.

Answer: *c.*

206. Some people are impulsive, while others are reserved.

    a. Too general

    b. Too specific

    c. Main idea

    d. Irrelevant

Answer: *d.* Irrelevant. This statement has nothing to do with the practicality of classifying personality traits.

207. Personalities cannot be sharply divided into dichotomized classifications.

    a. Too general

    b. Too specific

    c. Main idea

    d. Irrelevant

Answer: *c.* Main idea

208. The traits "sociable-seclusive" would be at opposite ends of a continuum measuring personality traits.

    a. Too general

    b. Too specific

    c. Main idea

    d. Irrelevant

Answer: *b.* Too specific. This is only one example given in the paragraph.

Of all the European nations, it was England that furnished the largest number of early settlers in the American colonies, and it was from English life, institutions, and historical experience that the basic institutions of American life were derived. The civilization established in the thirteen colonies either was English from the beginning or was to receive before the close of the seventeenth century a strong English flavor. Further, for over 150 years, the portion of colonial America from which the United States later developed was part of the British empire. These colonies were, because of this association, deeply influenced by developments that occurred in what was still the motherland.

209. For over 150 years part of America was a member of the British Empire.
   a. Too general
   b. Too specific
   c. Main idea
   d. Irrelevant

Answer: b. Too specific. This statement does not mention any effects of the close American-British association.

210. Despite the close relationship between the American colonies and Britain, the colonies revolted and formed an independent nation.
   a. Too general
   b. Too specific
   c. Main idea
   d. Irrelevant

Answer: d. Irrelevant. No mention is made in the paragraph of the eventual Revolutionary War.

211. Queen Elizabeth I ruled England during the period of the American colonization.
   a. Too general
   b. Too specific
   c. Main idea
   d. Irrelevant

Answer: d. Irrelevant. There is no mention in the paragraph of England's ruler at that time.

212. Which of the following is the main idea?
   a. The English people, customs, and way of life had a dominant influence on colonial America.
   b. Most early settlers in the American colonies were English.
   c. English influence in America has all but vanished in the past 150 years.
   d. The portion of colonial America from which the United States later developed was part of the British Empire.

Answer: a.

College students who eat all their meals at one of the college- or university-regulated food services are likely to be offered a well-balanced diet. The offering of well-balanced meals does not ensure, however, that the students make wise selections. In addition, many students eat their meals in restaurants or other public eating places where they may not be offered foods that provide all the nutrients needed by the body. College students, generally speaking, are well fed; few of them show extreme deficiency symptoms. Many students, on the other hand, are operating at a level below their achievement potential because of insufficiencies in their diet.

213. Students should try to eat lots of oranges and other citrus fruits.

The above summary is irrelevant because

a. It fails to mention the few students who show extreme deficiency symptoms.
b. Although the paragraph does mention proper diets, it does not mention a specific diet.
c. Not all college students eat at college- or university-regulated food services.
d. It is too vague concerning the place of vegetables and meat in a student's diet.

Answer: *b.*

214. Which of the following is the main idea?

a. Not all college students eat at college- or university-regulated food services.
b. In order to operate at peak achievement potential a college student must maintain a proper diet.
c. College- or university-regulated food services are generally good places to eat.
d. Most college students have the means available to maintain a proper diet, but not all of them do it.

Answer: *d.*

215. Most students who eat at college- or university-regulated food services eat healthy, well-balanced diets.

The above summary is too specific because

a. Not all these food services offer well-balanced diets.
b. Many students eat in restaurants.
c. Some students show extreme deficiency symptoms
d. The paragraph also discusses students who do not eat well-balanced diets.

Answer: *d.*

It is impossible to conceive of a modern society operating without benefit of law—without the carefully formulated rules which keep our intricate social fabric from coming apart at the seams. No rational person believes that the complex problems arising in an individual, urban society could be controlled except by means of law, courts, penalties, and policemen.

216. The complex problems arising in industry and commerce cannot be controlled without laws.
  The above summary is too specific because
  a. It fails to mention courts, penalties, and policemen.
  b. It deals with only two areas of life and ignores the more encompassing concept, i.e., modern society.
  c. It fails to mention how laws manage to control.
  d. The paragraph refers to only modern industry.

Answer: *b.*

217. Most people consider courts and policemen a necessity.
  a. Too general
  b. Too specific
  c. Main idea
  d. Irrelevant

Answer: *a.* Too general. The paragraph explains why it is impossible for a society to exist without laws.

218. **Which of the following is irrelevant?**
  a. All rational people believe that laws, courts, penalties, and policemen represent the best means of control in modern society.
  b. The laws in modern society are designed to uphold the rights of common man.
  c. Many problems arising in urban society would get completely out of hand were it not for the existence of many carefully formulated rules.
  d. It is difficult to imagine a modern society without laws.

Answer: *b.*

Locomotion [the ability to move about] serves not only in food catching, but also secondarily in numerous other animal activities. For example, locomotion plays a fundamental role in mate selection and in reproduction, functions which the mobile animal accomplishes far more readily than the sessile plant. Locomotion also is an important factor in protecting animals against environmental dangers, climatic changes in particular. For example, many animals carry out seasonal north-south migrations. Others remain at given latitudes permanently, yet through locomotion they are able to search out protective forests, caves, or self-constructed shelters like burrows, hives, nests, and houses.

219. Which of the following is too specific?

   a. Locomotion is important to animals because it plays an essential role in mate selection.
   b. The mobile animal is more readily fitted for survival than the sessile plant.
   c. Locomotion is of great importance to many animals.
   d. Mobile animals are more likely to carry out seasonal migrations than to build burrows, hives, nests, etc.

Answer: a.

220. Which of the following is the main idea?

   a. Locomotion protects animals from environmental dangers.
   b. Locomotion provides the means for animals to carry out many important functions.
   c. Locomotion is of primary importance only in food catching.
   d. Locomotion is the only important factor in the survival of any given animal.

Answer: b.

221. Locomotion protects animals from environmental dangers.

   The above summary is too specific because

   a. It fails to mention how locomotion protects.
   b. It fails to distinguish between primary and secondary functions of locomotion.
   c. It mentions only one function of locomotion.
   d. It fails to mention the functional equivalent to locomotion in sessile plants.

Answer: c.

We all use "commonsense psychology" as we struggle along from day to day. We try to understand other people. We attempt to predict what this or that person will do next. Most of us have plenty of ideas about how to get control over our own lives and sometimes over the lives of others. In other words, each of us has commonsense psychological "theories" of our own—the best approach for raising children, selling a car, making friends, attracting members of the opposite sex, impressing people, controlling anger.

222. Which of the following is irrelevant?
   a. Most people have a theory about the best way to raise children.
   b. "Commonsense psychology" is used by all of us.
   c. The theories of "commonsense psychology" are always wrong.
   d. Each of us has commonsense psychological "theories."

Answer: c.

223. Which of the following is too specific?
   a. Most people have a commonsense theory about how to raise children.
   b. "Commonsense psychology" is used by scientists as well as by the average person.
   c. Commonsense theories are usually wrong.
   d. Commonsense theories are usually right.

Answer: a.

224. Before looking at the answer below, try to state for yourself the main idea of this paragraph.

Main Idea: *We all use "commonsense psychology" theories in our everyday life.*

The theories of Sigmund Freud (1856–1939) . . . are widely accepted by the public—so widely accepted that many people equate psychology with *psychoanalytic theory* (the general name for Freud's theories about personality, abnormality, and treatment). Psychoanalytic theory is, however, only one psychological theory.

225. Which of the following is irrelevant?

   a. Freud's theories are widely accepted by the public.
   b. Psychoanalytic theory is the general name for Freud's theories.
   c. Sigmund Freud was a Viennese physician.
   d. Psychoanalytic theory is only one of many psychological theories.

Answer: c.

226. Which of the following is too specific?
   a. Sigmund Freud became famous by treating neurotics.
   b. Freud had no theories about personality.
   c. Freud's theories are not very widely accepted by the public.
   d. Psychoanalytic theory is the general name for Freud's theories.

Answer: d.

227. Before looking at the answer given below, try to state for yourself the main idea of this paragraph.

Main Idea: *Although Sigmund Freud's psychoanalytic theory is widely accepted and often equated with psychology, it is only one of many psychological theories.*

Review

A. A statement which summarized only the ideas contained in the topic sentence would be marked _____.

Answer: *Too specific.*

B. A statement which extended beyond the limits of the specific topic under discussion in a paragraph would be marked _____.

Answer: *Too general.*

C. A statement which was incomplete or which dealt with only some of the specific ideas covered in the paragraph would be marked _____.

Answer: *Too specific.*

D. A statement would be marked _____ if it contained ideas which were not actually part of the paragraph.

Answer: *Irrelevant.*

E. For a paragraph about volcanic lava a statement about all rock layers would be marked _____.

Answer: *Too general.*

F. For a paragraph about various breeds of hunting dogs a statement about Irish Setters would be marked _____.

Answer: *Too specific.*

G. For a paragraph about modern aircraft a statement which concentrated on the first successful flight of the Wright brothers would be marked either _____ or _____, depending on whether or not this flight was mentioned in the paragraph.

Answer: *Irrelevant or too specific.*

H. Define the term "main idea" as used in these exercises.

Answer: *The main idea is a statement which summarizes the ideas contained in the topic sentence and supporting sentences of a paragraph.*

Part 6:
Stating the Main Idea

From here on you are on your own as far as summarizing paragraphs is concerned. You are to write a statement of the main idea in your own words; then compare it with the one in the book. Be sure to remember that the main idea is to cover both the topic sentence and the important and relevant support information.

You will not be able to score your answers as absolutely right or wrong in this section. If you feel that it is difficult for you to tell whether your answer is an adequate statement of the main idea, you might try consulting the teacher or some other qualified person.

Studies of large groups of babies show that during the first three to four months of life all babies are ambidextrous—that is, they use both hands, with no preference for one or the other. By the middle of the first year, however, definite signs of hand preference appear.

Main Idea: *Although babies are ambidextrous during the first three or four months of life, definite signs of hand preference appear by the middle of the first year.*

Even for those energies to which a sense organ responds, no sense organ is infinitely sensitive. Each sense organ requires some minimum energy for stimulation. There are sounds that are too soft to be heard, light that is too faint to be seen, weights that are too light to be felt, and movements that are too slight to be detected. In a word, every sense has its absolute threshold. This is the minimum stimulus energy to which it can respond.

Main Idea: *Every sense organ has a minimum stimulus energy to which it can respond which is called its absolute threshold.*

Moonlight is really sunlight reflected to the earth from the surface of the moon. Moonlight often seems very bright to us. Looking over a landscape illuminated by the full moon, we exclaim, "Why, it's as bright as day!" Actual measurements show that moonlight is only $\frac{1}{400,000}$ as bright as sunlight. Owing to its irregular surface, the moon makes a poor reflector, reflecting only about seven per cent of the sun's light that falls on it. The full moon looks bright in the sky at night, but when we see it during the day while the sun is shining, its disk is so faint that we might easily mistake it for a patch of cloud.

Main Idea: *Moonlight is sunlight reflected to the earth from the surface of the moon; but since the surface of the moon is irregular, only a small amount of the sun's light is reflected.*

The color of a star is determined entirely by its temperature. We know that the higher the temperature of a body the brighter it appears. Not only does a body become brighter as its temperature rises but its color changes also. A piece of iron at low temperature glows a dull red. Heat it up and its color becomes cherry red, orange, yellow, until finally we say it is white-hot. Similarly, the tungsten filament in an electric-light globe shines with a bright white light because it is much hotter than the carbon filament in an old-fashioned light globe, which was at a much lower temperature and so was yellowish in color. Similarly the stars appear different colors because they are at different temperatures.

Main Idea: *The color of a star is determined entirely by its temperature.*

Let us suppose that the earth had a homogeneous surface: a surface either all water or all land of uniform character and altitude. Let us suppose further that the earth did not rotate but that the direct rays of the sun nevertheless reached all points on the equator at all seasons. Under such conditions the air movement would be very simple. The air near the equator would expand, would overflow, and the cooler air of higher latitudes would crowd under it, forcing it aloft. At or near the earth's surface, the winds in the northern hemisphere would be north winds; those in the southern hemisphere would be south winds. At higher altitudes, the directions of the winds would be the opposite of those at the surface.

Main Idea: *If the earth had a homogeneous surface and did not rotate, then the winds near the earth's surface in the Northern Hemisphere would be north winds and those in the Southern Hemisphere would be south winds, and at higher altitudes the wind would blow in the opposite directions.*

What is meant by normal? It is important to understand the term, since it is so frequently used to describe the condition of the mentally healthy individual. In one sense, "normal" is a synonym for "typical." This is a statistical use of the word, meaning that an individual is average compared with group norms. The classic example is that of the individual whose height and weight are considered normal because he is average in height and weight for his age.

Main Idea: *One of the meanings for the word "normal" is "typical" or, in statistical terms, that an individual is average compared with group norms.*

Every reaction to a stimulus requires a finite amount of time, and the time between stimulus and response is called reaction time. For simple reflexes, this time is of the order of $\frac{1}{10}$ second, though it varies with the reflex. For simple voluntary reactions, such as pushing a key when a light is flashed or a bell is sounded, the reaction time is roughly $\frac{2}{10}$ second. For more complex reactions, such as pushing the brake pedal on an automobile, reaction time is closer to one second.

Main Idea: *Reaction time is the amount of time between stimulus and response, and the length ot time may vary from $\frac{1}{10}$ second for simple reflexes to 1 second for complex reactions.*

Aphasia is the general term for language disorders. It usually occurs when some damage to the speech areas of the brain causes a person to forget or become unable to handle language as he previously did. The damage may be a bullet wound or other head injury, or it may be a result of a cerebral hemorrhage, that is, a cerebral vascular accident (CVA) or stroke. It can also occur in senile aging, as the brain deteriorates.

Main Idea: *Aphasia is the general term for speech disorders that are usually caused by damage to the speech areas of the brain.*

The markings that make up the rather blurred features of the "man in the moon" are simply regions on the lunar surface that are darker than the rest. Early astronomers, such as Galileo and others who followed him, were unable to see these dark areas distinctly with their small, imperfect telescopes, so they called them maria (seas) because they thought them actual bodies of water. Today we know that the moon has no air or water on its surface, but the names given to these dark areas have been retained, and we still speak of the moon's Sea of Serenity, Sea of Tranquility, and Ocean of Storms.

Main Idea: *Although early astronomers believed the "man in the moon" was caused by seas on the moon, it is known today that the moon has no air or water.*

Of the various materials the plant gets from its environment none is more important than water. The very composition of plants attests this, most herbaceous plants being made up of seventy to eighty-five per cent water and even woody parts of plants consisting of as much as fifty per cent water. Algae and other water plants frequently contain ninety-five to ninety-eight per cent water. Moreover, plants growing in soil are constantly losing large quantities of water by transpiration. This water must be supplied through absorption by the roots if wilting of the plant is to be prevented. Water, being the most important solvent in nature, is the medium by which inorganic substances and elaborated foods are transported from one part of the plant to another. Without a constant supply of water the plant could not carry on any of its physiological activities such as photosynthesis, digestion, respiration, and growth.

Main Idea: *Water is one of the most important substances which plants receive from their environment, for without it the plant's physiological activities would be impossible.*

Experiments done earlier in the century led to the conclusion that the source of the hunger drive is stomach contractions—when the stomach contracts, the drive is initiated. This is the *local-stimulus theory* of hunger. But more recent work has shown that the relationship between stomach contractions and hunger is weak at best.

Main Idea: *Early experiments supported the local-stimulus theory of hunger, which holds that hunger is caused by stomach contractions but recent experiments do not support this theory.*

Frictional forces play an important role in mechanics. . . . Unlike the weight of a body, which is constant at any particular location, the frictional force between a body and a surface depends on many factors. For example, when a heavy block of wood is pushed along the top of a table, the amount of frictional resistance depends on the surface of the table, the surface of the block, how clean the surfaces are, the speed of the block, and the forces pressing the surfaces together. When a body moves on a surface, there is always . . . resistance to the motion.

Main Idea: *Frictional forces resist the motion of a body moving on a surface, and the strength of this resistance depends on many factors.*

Comets with their luminous heads and tails, are among the most interesting members of our solar system. The heads are probably composed of swarms of meteor-like bodies and the tails consist of tiny particles driven away from the heads by the pressure of light from the sun. Some comets enter our solar system from outer space, move around the sun . . . and speed away never to return; while others . . . come back at regular intervals.

Main Idea: *Comets are composed of a head which probably consists of swarms of meteor-like bodies and a tail of tiny particles driven away from the head by the pressure of light from the sun. Some pass the earth only once; others return at regular intervals.*

Another very common obstacle to the child's acquiring of skills is the adult's fear that the child will hurt himself when trying new skills. Because of this fear that the child will have an accident, the adult checks the child's adventuresome tendency and he may keep him from experimenting, from trying to learn, or from doing the things that would help him to learn how to control his body.

Main Idea: *An adult's fear for a child's safety may prevent the child from experimenting or from trying to do those things which will lead to learning bodily control.*

When informal sanctions fail, the ultimate punishment that society visits upon the rebel is force—physical torture, banishment, or death. In one or more forms force is used by all societies to control those who have most flagrantly or persistently violated the moral norms. . . . The type of force wielded by human society is always a collective act. . . . Force is applied by legitimate, vested authority, in the name of a group or the total society.

Main Idea: *When informal sanctions fail, society uses force to keep order.*

If we listen to any music by one of the late baroque masters, a chorus by Johann Sebastian Bach, an aria by Georg Friedrich Handel, or a concerto movement by Antonio Vivaldi, we are struck by the greater sense of breadth and purpose which this music has over comparable works by earlier composers. This music seems to reach farther and to achieve its goals with more telling force than any music heretofore composed. We cannot help being impressed by the structural grandeur of late baroque music, fully realized in works of broad scope, but also reflected in the small compositions of this era.

Main Idea: *All the music of the late baroque period has a greater sense of breadth and purpose than any of the preceding period.*

Has the end to the feasible size reduction of computer circuitry been reached? Hardly. The boards of today will become the tiny chips of tomorrow. One scientist has speculated that . . . it may be possible to achieve the packing density currently obtained on a square inch *throughout a cubic inch* of material. The density of electronic components would then be "about a fourth the density of nerve cells in the human brain." Thus, it is expected that . . . central processors with the power of today's large computers will occupy the space of a shoebox!

Main Idea: *Computers with a given capacity will continue to get smaller.*

The great number of significant events that have occurred during the vast length of recorded geologic time has made it of particular importance for geologists to devise a system of organizing these events into a systematic way according to their respective time relations. The geologic time scale has been devised for this purpose. Although the divisions are somewhat arbitrary, this scale has proved to be quite satisfactory.

Main Idea: *The geologic time scale was developed in order to have a way of organizing significant geologic events.*

An especially clear example of action by both state and Federal governments to discourage competition is found in the so-called "fair-trade" laws. These laws permit manufacturers of a large variety of drugstore merchandise, books, liquor, jewelry, cigar, electrical appliances, sporting goods, and many other items to specify either the minimum or the exact price at which their products may be sold by retailers.

Main Idea: *Fair-trade laws are an attempt by government to discourage competition by permitting manufacturers of certain items to specify either the minimum or the exact price at which their products may be sold by retailers.*

From the scientific point of view, the lack of written records in America has been a far from unmixed evil. With no inscriptions to search for or decipher, American investigators have turned to a steady improvement of archaeological methods, especially as these apply to dating the past. Although scientific archaeology originated in Europe, American methods of excavation and recording have become as good as any in the Old World, and our scientists have contributed at least two dating techniques more exact than any developed abroad. One of these employs the varying annual growth in tree rings as a clue to the age of structures in which wood or even charcoal has been found. It has made possible the establishment of culture sequences in southwestern United States.

Main Idea: *The lack of written records in America has resulted in the development of dating techniques using the varying widths of tree rings.*

American civilization, as we have seen, was the offspring of Europe, inheriting a mixture of its characteristics and closely resembling it in fundamental traits. Institutions of government in America owed a particular debt to English accomplishment. But American civilization was not wholly a product of Europe. The primitive coast of North America was a different environment, and some of the beliefs and practices transplanted from Europe took root and flourished while others died. The American frontier chose some elements of European culture for survival and others for destruction. Between Old World culture and New World conditions there was an interaction out of which American society grew.

Main Idea: *Although America inherited many of its characteristics from Europe, the different environment in North America resulted in the destruction of some of the elements of European culture.*

Compared with North America and Northwestern Europe, Central Eastern Asia is faced with a general inadequacy of known resources for large-scale industrial development. There is limited variety in the more important deposits of mineral resources. A few minerals are concentrated overwhelmingly in a few districts within the region; most of this mineral wealth, for example, is found in China. Japan has the only large stands of accessible forest resources in the region. China alone has large arable land resources, but because of the large population, that country resembles the others in having only small units of cultivable land per capita.

Main Idea: *Compared with North America and Europe, Central Eastern Asia has few resources for large-scale industrial development and agriculture.*

Damage to the brain of a growing human being can be a causal factor in an almost infinitely long list of behavioral abnormalities. The damage may result in relatively circumscribed deficits in sensorimotor abilities which are hardly noticeable in the everyday functioning of the child. At the other extreme, it may involve complicated emerging functions in the intellectual and personality spheres, thereby wreaking havoc with the child's ability to cope with everyday problems and his capacity to share congenial relationships with other persons.

Main Idea: *Brain damage in children can cause many behavioral abnormalities which may be minor or severe.*

Beginning in 1929, the American people were plunged violently from the complacent dream of "the final victory over poverty" into the severest test of their courage and endurance, and of the stability of American institutions, since the Civil War. Their experiences during the bitter years of the Great Depression left a mark on the nation which was to last for decades. America's politics and her social and economic institutions were to be profoundly altered by this experience.

Main Idea: *The depression of 1929 provided a severe test of the stability of American institutions and of the courage and endurance of the American people, and both were profoundly altered by it.*

A Final Note to the Student

Congratulations! You have finished the main idea exercises. It is hoped that you will now be very skilled at interpreting paragraphs. As we said in the beginning, however, this is not all there is to being a good reader. A good reader is also able to do the following:

1. Understand and use details
2. Discover the organization of material
3. Read to recognize and use scientific principles
4. Use study-type reading materials to prepare for examinations
5. Skim over material rapidly to get a general view of it before reading more carefully
6. Scan material rapidly to find specific facts
7. Read critically, evaluating the author's bias, tone, and reliability and assessing his conclusions
8. Most important of all, do all the above things rapidly and efficiently and retain the information gained

This book is part of a large series of basic-skill-development materials. Other parts of the series are designed to improve other reading skills. (Some parts also deal with spelling, studying, vocabulary, arithmetic, and writing.) You may want to use some of them, too.